DEEP DISH CONVERSATIONS

T0274698

DEEP DISH
CONVERSATIONS

VOICES OF SOCIAL CHANGE IN NASHVILLE

JEROME MOORE

VANDERBILT UNIVERSITY PRESS
Nashville, Tennessee

Copyright 2023 by Jerome Moore

Published 2023 by Vanderbilt University Press

All rights reserved

First printing 2023

Library of Congress Cataloging-in-Publication Data

Names: Moore, Jerome Lamont, 1990– author.
Title: Deep dish conversations : voices of social change in Nashville /
  Jerome Moore.
Description: Nashville, Tennessee : Vanderbilt University Press, 2023. |
  Includes bibliographical references.
Identifiers: LCCN 2022061366 (print) | LCCN 2022061367 (ebook) | ISBN
  9780826505774 (paperback) | ISBN 9780826505781 (epub) | ISBN
  9780826505798 (pdf)
Subjects: LCSH: Social change—Tennessee—Nashville. |
  Equality—Tennessee—Nashville. | Racism—Tennessee—Nashville. |
  Nashville (Tenn.)—Social conditions—21st century.
Classification: LCC HN80.N2 M66 2023 (print) | LCC HN80.N2 (ebook) | DDC
  303.409768/55—dc23/eng/20230210
LC record available at https://lccn.loc.gov/2022061366
LC ebook record available at https://lccn.loc.gov/2022061367

*To all the individuals who have dared
to venture beyond the familiar and explore the unknown,
even in the face of discouragement.*

CONTENTS

FOREWORD

DR. SEKOU FRANKLIN

Jerome Moore's *Deep Dish Conversations* uses storytelling to examine Nashville in the twenty-first century. Storytelling comes in many forms: religious discourse, musical and literary expressions, protests, politics, and economic boosterism. In this book, storytelling embodies interviews with leading activists, intellectuals, and public officials, who share their thoughts on justice, transformational change, and inclusion.

To some extent, this book is an investigation of race and systemic policies that disadvantage Black and Brown residents in Nashville. Yet, it is also an exposé on place-making in a pro-growth, southern city networked to a global economy. Place-making describes how urban residents, workers, activists, intellectuals, and public officials establish new identities and hold on to existing ones. It investigates the built environments—old and new—such as the expanded or diminished housing stock, commercial development, and neighborhoods structured by an investor class, racial segregation, police-community relations, and workplace stability.[1]

Trademarks have best characterized place-making and cultural identity in Nashville: Buckle of the Bible Belt, Music City, and Athens of the South. Today, Nashville is called the "It City," as described a decade ago by Kim Severson in the *New York Times*.[2] The city and the surrounding counties are permanent destinations for northern and west coast migrants and high-value businesses seeking to find the new promised land of low taxes, southern cosmopolitanism, and a creative class.

However, the emergence of the It City raises questions about livability for residents at the bottom of the opportunity structure. How do working-class and low-wealth residents create a sense of belonging in a city that looks increasingly unfamiliar to them? How do residents confront the daily burdens of economic distress, wage suppression, austerity, neoliberal policies, and land-use deregulation? How do communities victimized by generations of hyper-incarceration find stability in the new Nashville? How do poor peoples' movements advance equity-based policies in a city burdened by a fragmented political system that privileges powerful business interests? And where do working-class residents find affordable places to live if the cost of rent and housing has outpaced the rise in wages?

These questions are addressed in *Deep Dish Conversations*. Although the contributors arrive at different answers to the questions, each one extends a mirror to the readers to compel them/us to position equity at the forefront of place-making. By doing this, concerns about race, place-making, and resilience are tethered to Moore's constant search for accountability and resolution to these complicated questions.

I first met Moore a decade ago when he was a student at Middle Tennessee State University. Despite the professor-student relationship, we were bound by a common thread. I lived in North Nashville—or "Out Norf" as local people called it—near his stomping ground of Pearl-Cohn High School. MTSU is only thirty-five minutes from North Nashville, but the two locations seem like opposite sides of the country. When I met Moore, gentrification had not taken hold of his community in North Nashville. The identities, rhythm, and ethos of the area's working-class neighborhoods captured the essence of Black Nashville.

Notwithstanding our shared citizenship, I was not raised in the city. Unlike my immediate neighbors, I benefitted from a middle-class positionality. As an outsider, I leaned on Black students from North Nashville for information. My relationship with them was dialectical. I taught them political science, and they became my urban griots, regularly updating me about "street" politics in the community.

After graduating from MTSU, Moore joined the Peace Corps and moved to Paraguay. Once his tour concluded, he collaborated with community development initiatives in China, the Philippines, and Costa Rica. Along the way, he returned to Nashville to assist grassroots organizations such as *The Contributor*, a newspaper that represents the unhoused/houseless community. Based on these collective experiences, he created a community development framework that fuses grassroots organizing, racial justice, and international education.

Deep Dish Conversations captures Moore's dedication to organizing and equity. It is just the latest publication about race, social class, and survival in Nashville. The Brookings Institution has produced two reports since 2018 that highlight Blacks in North Nashville. More recently, Steve Haruch's *Greetings from New Nashville: How a Sleepy Southern Town Became "It" City* (2020), *Praying with Our Feet: Pursuing Justice and Healing on the Streets* (2021) by Lindsey Krinks, and Amie Thurber and Learotha Williams Jr.'s edited volume *I'll Take You There: Exploring Nashville's Social Justice Sites* (2021) provide refreshing accounts of Nashville in the twenty-first century.

Moore interviews thirteen influencers working on different fronts. The first section looks at Blacks who grew up in North Nashville at a time when the neighborhood was more than 90 percent Black. Jamel Campbell-Gooch and Joshua Black discuss growing up in a community shaped by Black businesses and colleges and universities yet plagued by unemployment and hyper-incarceration.

North Nashville has garnered national attention due to the previously mentioned Brookings' studies. During Campbell-Gooch and Black's formative years, the neighborhoods encompassing the 37208 area code had the highest incarceration rate in the country.[3] The expansion of prisons, draconian sentencing laws, over-policing, and aggressive prosecution made North Nashville ground zero for the nationwide expansion of the carceral state.

The second section of the book, "Life in Prison," chronicles life through the lenses of Calvin "Fridge" Bryant, Rahim Buford, and Theeda Murphy. The men grew up in communities plagued by over-policing—Buford in northeast Nashville and Bryant in the southside's Edgehill public housing development. Both became community advocates after serving long prison sentences. Murphy is a police and prison abolitionist. She has also been a leading advocate for mental health justice.

Buford has spent his post-incarceration years leading Unheard Voices Outreach, an organization that advocates on behalf of formerly incarcerated persons. He also managed the Nashville Community Bail Fund for several years. Bryant was a high-profile target of the Drug-Free School Zones Act that was aimed at high-poverty neighborhoods from the mid-1990s to 2020. In addition to speaking against zero-tolerance policies, he created the Positive Inner-City Kids (PICK) foundation. Murphy's most recent work is as the co-director of No Exceptions Prison Collective, an organization that works on sentencing reform and advocates for the closing of prisons in Tennessee.

Governance is the theme of section three. Moore interviews Christiane Buggs of the Metropolitan Nashville Board of Education, former Public Defender Dawn Deaner, and Juvenile Court Judge Sheila Calloway. Buggs provides insight on educational justice and community control of MNPS. She calls for an investment of monetary resources in low- and moderate-income schools, as well as community control of neighborhood schools. Her commentary raises an important concern. Although neighborhoods are diversifying due to gentrification, many white parents are intentionally choosing to avoid neighborhood and Black-populated schools.

Deaner and Calloway discuss the challenges with ameliorating injustices in institutions anchored by rules, procedures, and policies that have penalized poor people for generations. Abuse, family disarray, food insecurity, and adverse childhood experiences create additional barriers for people trapped in the criminal and juvenile justice systems.

City officials created restorative justice and decarceration programs to counter these problems. These include a client advisory board, a participatory defense project, workload reductions, community mediation, and a parental assistance program. Although these initiatives have not radically transformed the criminal justice and juvenile justice systems, their advocacy approach is a significant departure from that of their predecessors. A decade earlier, the previous generation of district attorneys, public defenders, juvenile court, and criminal courts bolstered the carceral state and its reach into poor neighborhoods.

The book's fourth section describes why white influencers must challenge racism in Nashville. The contributors, Tim Wise and William Acuff, spent their lives working in anti-racism struggles. Wise is a nationally renowned author and commentator on white privilege. Acuff is the co-founder of Corner to Corner, a faith-based organization that serves at-risk youth. Both men believe in racial and economic justice—a commitment borne out of family upbringing and childhood experiences.

Public safety is the last section in the book. Moore interviews Captain Carlos Lara, the Chief Diversity Officer in the Metropolitan Nashville Police Department; Marcus Trotter-Lockett and Emma Crownover of Safer Schools Nashville; and Jorge Salles Diaz, an organizer in law school who became an immigrant rights' attorney.

Lara and the Safer Schools Nashville activists provide competing views of public safety. Lara believes MNPD has been moving in the right direction since the wave of Black Lives Matter / I Can't Breathe protests of 2020. He points to the diversity and community engagement initiatives implemented by Chief John Drake a year later. He defends the use of School Resource Officers (SROs) and supports Metro Nashville Council's substantial budget allocation to MNPD.

On the other hand, Trotter-Lockett and Crownover insist that public dollars are best spent divesting from MNPD and redirecting resources to restorative and youth leadership programs. They insist upon the removal of police officers from schools. In place of SROs, they urge the Metro Nashville Council and school board to heavily invest in social and emotional learning programs.

The last part of this section makes the connection between public safety and economic security. Diaz explains why wage theft is rampant in Nashville. Wage theft is the denial or underpayment of contractual wages to marginal workers such as the undocumented, houseless/unhoused, and formerly incarcerated. It is systemic in the construction and hospitality industries, or any unregulated industry dominated by powerful contractors and subcontractors. Ameliorating wage theft and economic insecurity, Diaz insists, will require a "multiracial movement" that unites Brown and Black workers.

Even though Nashville is a cosmopolitan city, this book provides a sobering account of racial and economic injustices. In the book, we discover how the criminal justice system and policing practices made their best attempt to ruin a generation of Black people. We learn how a deregulated construction industry encourages wage theft. We are forced to consider how racism is still a facet of everyday place-making in the city.

Despite these challenges, *Deep Dish Conversations* celebrates human agency and the power of everyday people and public officials to make change in the face of insurmountable odds. Change is hard to come by, but it can happen. Public officials can rearrange institutions and leverage their reputational resources to implement reforms—whether incremental or transformative. Resistance movements and activists are not bound to nostalgic reflections about the civil rights struggles of the 1950s and 1960s. They are vehicles for shifting contemporary agendas and political culture. Intellectuals, movement lawyers, and entertainers can shape public discourse and speak truth to power.

This book will inspire new investigations of race and place-making in Nashville and the Middle Tennessee region. It will encourage scholars and activists to tell more stories about the It City through multiple expressions and platforms. It also lays the groundwork for more reflective conversations that can provide insight about the social, political, and economic transformations of the urban South.

NOTES

1. Deborah Martin, "'Place-Framing' as Place-Making: Constituting a Neighborhood for Organizing and Activism," *Annuals of the Association of American Geographers* 93, no. 3 (2003): 730–50; Sarah Elwood, Victoria Lawson, and Samuel Nowak, "Middle-Class Poverty Politics: Making Place, Making People," *Annuals of the Association of American Geographers* 105, no. 1 (2015): 123–43.

2. Kim Severson, "Nashville's Latest Big Hit Could Be the City Itself," *New York Times*, January 8, 2013, https://www.nytimes.com/2013/01/09/us/nashville-takes-its-turn-in-the-spotlight.html.

3. Adam Looney and Nicholas Turner, *Work and Opportunity Before and After Incarceration* (Washington, DC: Brookings Institution, 2018), 4, 17.

INTRODUCTION

WE ARE ALL AFFECTED by the social, cultural, and political issues facing our community: white supremacy, racism, anti-Semitism, poverty, housing, education, anti-Blackness, gender equality, policing. And if these issues affect us all, then we should all be talking about them—together. The conversations can and will be tense and uncomfortable, but we must learn to lean into the tension and get comfortable being uncomfortable if we really want to address and reconstruct the problems that affect us all—albeit on different levels.

I started *Deep Dish Conversations* to explore perspectives of social change through conversations with leaders and members of the Nashville community.

I have had the opportunity to build community power with respected community-based organizations throughout Nashville, Tennessee, and in international settings like Paraguay, Costa Rica, China, and the Philippines. This unique journey helped me understand the value and importance of engaging with people outside of my own community bubble. Once we do that, we not only open ourselves to learn about other communities, but we also garner new perspective on how and why we are all variously affected by the critical issues that appear in every community.

As a native of Nashville, I didn't grow up knowing much about other communities in my city. I needed to keep exploring with intention and to cultivate cultural awareness and acceptance that would help break down barriers. I needed to interact meaningfully with people of different backgrounds, ideas, and lived experiences, and I needed a brave space to do that. *Deep Dish Conversations* created an intentional, civil, brave space for our community to engage and learn through daring conversations about difficult issues and about what actions we might take to build a more just and equitable Nashville.

This book is a powerful and comprehensive exploration of a wide range of social justice issues, offering an in-depth analysis of different perspectives and topics. By incorporating diverse viewpoints, the book sheds light on the lived experiences of individuals from varied backgrounds, providing valuable insights into the complexities and nuances of these issues. Through its discussions, the book highlights the pressing need for systemic change to create a more equitable and just society. It effectively emphasizes the urgency of addressing the root causes of these issues and the importance of collective action to bring about meaningful change. The conversations that form the basis of this book were held at the now defunct Gino's East Nashville and the Deep Dish Conversations studio.

The individuals who make up each section reflect what many of our communities are made of. As you are introduced, try to identify them with people in your own community. How do you know them or why don't you? What type of relationship do you have with that person? How do you support them? You can put a face and a voice to each interviewee by scanning the QR code attached to each section to watch the full interviews.

These conversations are intended to educate and enlighten, as well as help generate a measurable and workable list of actions that our city might take to build more just and equitable communities. Use these conversations as a tool to reflect and grow, to expand your own diversity of thought around these critical and pressing topics. Learn from the stories of people with experiences and perspectives from outside of your own bubble. As these conversations are happening over pizza, we should remember to make sure every community member has a fair and equitable chance to get the slice of pizza they desire from the enormous pie that we all help prepare.

There has never been a more necessary time to unpack what the hell is going on in our world today. It is my hope that you, the reader, will create or get involved in more conversations that allow and welcome the exploration of all perspectives on social change from community members. It is easy for us to be in community with only those who think or even look like we do. But these conversations will flourish, and will reach even broader segments of our community and beyond, if we become more intentional about really exploring the diversity of thought that exists in our entire community ecosystem. Having a conversation does not mean perspectives will change, but one can learn to understand *why* someone has a particular perspective from simply listening. We are all affected by the social, cultural, and political environment we share, but many of us may be waiting for a space to articulate our perspective on its causes, effects, and solutions.

PART I

WE THE NORTH

CHAPTER ONE

JAMEL CAMPBELL-GOOCH

Jamel Campbell-Gooch is a Nashville native and community organizer whose work is rooted in 37208 but touches every part of Nashville. As we explore North Nashville with Jamel, reflect on the historically Black communities in your city. How have they been treated over time? Have you taken the time to learn about them? Are you welcomed in those neighborhoods? What implicit bias have you had about those communities?

As a violence interrupter, Jamel provided community students and school staff with information that helped to change how youth think and feel about violence and enhanced interpersonal and emotional skills like communication and problem-solving, empathy, and conflict management.

He co-founded both the Black Nashville Assembly, which is building a bold and Black political agenda and organizing to transform Nashville, and of Moving Nashville Forward, which demonstrates how a guaranteed basic income can eliminate poverty, disrupt conditions that reinforce poverty, and create healthier communities. He was a member of Nashville's Community Oversight Board, which was created by voters in 2018 to hold police accountable.

Keep in mind that the topics at the center of this conversation are not unique to Nashville but are reflected in many Black communities throughout cities in the United States.

MOORE: What conditions are you trying to change?

CAMPBELL-GOOCH: If you take a snapshot in any part of history, there's usually adversity happening in North Nashville. My experience in North Nashville, when I was growing up on Clay Street, is I realized we had a shit ton of dead ends that didn't make sense. On the end of those dead ends is the interstate. When the city decided to build that interstate right there, they displaced over 620 Black homes, over 50 Black businesses, over 25 rooming houses, and destroyed over 25 Black churches.

MOORE: That interstate stretches through Jefferson Street, where all of those HBCUs are. Peculiar that they put the interstate right through the thriving heart of the Black culture in Nashville.

CAMPBELL-GOOCH: Not just the heart of Black Nashville, it's really the soul of the entire city. Everything that Nashville is known for can be directly tied to North Nashville. Whether it's being known as the Music City, tied directly to the Jubilee Singers singing around the world, the It City, the Progressive City, tied to student activism during the Civil Rights Movement, even hot chicken, tied directly to Prince's Hot Chicken.

So we're not just talking about an area of North Nashville that is rooted in being Black here. You're also talking about the people that define the culture of the city.

The conditions I'm trying to change are all directly tied to poverty. The way we've treated North Nashville has created a condition where poverty is rampant, and usually where you have poverty rampant you have violence, you have all of these other social ills. But the beautiful thing about North Nashville is we can fix it. In North Nashville we can fix it, anywhere across Tennessee, period.

MOORE: For those who might not know, what are those dead ends that you're talking about?

CAMPBELL-GOOCH: Excuse me if I'm wrong, but I'm thinking about streets like Scovel and Underwood. The reason why none of the avenues connecting Nashville curve is because there's an interstate through the middle of them. So when we talk about traffic all the time being an issue, no one ever really brings up the fact that the reason that we have a traffic problem is because the people who were in power, making the city plan and building the city infrastructure, were racist and anti-Black. So they made a decision based on that, and what we're seeing at this point is how a decision made in that type of evil and dogged and unrighteous ideology will harm everyone in the city. Everyone has to deal with that traffic shit. And the reason is because they decided to drive an interstate directly through the heart of North Nashville.

MOORE: How was it for you growing up on Clay Street and in North Nashville? How was your childhood?

CAMPBELL-GOOCH: That's a convoluted question because the adults around me, the tribe, my family, my folks in North Nashville made sure I had a very stable foundation. So I realized a lot of things after the fact, when I started leaving North Nashville. That's when I started broadening my horizon. I didn't know there was a such thing as a twenty-four-hour grocery store until I left North Nashville. Because on my streets everything closed at 8:00. Kroger's, everything. Walmart, Walgreens. It was a ghost town after 8:00. So I remember when I first got to TSU and I had met a brother that was from Franklin. I went out there to visit his parents' house. I remember like, seeing the grocery stores being twenty-four hours and, like, "Yo, is this normal type of shit?" So small things like that.

We used to have police officers literally just speeding up and down Clay Street at all times of night. I remember at one point, my next door neighbors had a raid executed on their home and I didn't know what was going on. The adults around me were able to navigate those social ills in a way that it would just seem like these were normal things. "We going to be resilient."

I remember realizing like, "Nah, this was specifically planned this way. North Nashville is a dead end." If you look at it on the map, you can only get to Bordeaux one way right across the highway, and you can only get out of it a couple of different ways, but there's only three ways to get out of North Nashville. So when a city is building like that, putting Black folks on an island, then it's like the issues that I saw going up—poverty, economic deprivation, schools that don't have enough books to go around, overcrowded classrooms, not enough housing, drugs, police everywhere—none of that stuff was normal, but when I grew up, we just navigated it.

MOORE: Because you think it's normal, you get conditioned to it.

CAMPBELL-GOOCH: For sure. I remember telling somebody for the first time that I was pulled over twenty-eight times. I started working at Foot Locker. That's where I got my first job, so I would have to go 65, get off at Metro Center, and go down back ways. You know, you can either go to Bordeaux or you can go down Clarksville Highway to get to Clay Street. At the time the chief, I think it was Chief Surpass, had an initiative called Nashville Safe Streets, where they flooded areas with police officers with the idea of deterring crime. So they would run into areas between 9:30 and 3 a.m. right in the pocket when a mall closes. So when I'm driving through, I'm hitting like, every single block, police officer, police officer, police officer. I was getting pulled over so many times that at one point—and I'm not getting tickets, just checking my ID—at some point they were just like, "We know him, he's getting off of work." They just kept letting me go, but the idea that I'm getting pulled over so much, they're having to run my license just from going to work. Things like that I thought were normal until I became a man and realized that it was intentionally planned that way.

MOORE: It's wild how those experiences affect you going forward but you don't realize them in the moment.

CAMPBELL-GOOCH: What's wild to me is how our systems of accountability center punishment. They don't center the harm. They center how much time you get. How long you going to be suspended from school. How much your fine going to be. They're not centering, "Okay, relationships were harmed here, how can we repair their harm?" It's fundamentally not set up to where you can get your harm repaired. We socialize our children through in-school suspension, out-of-school suspension, expulsion, to experience accountability in a way that is harmful to them. So if you got a student that's been experiencing in-school suspension or out-of-school suspension for years, when they get out, it's going to be normal, "I'm used to this." Even if you talk about what we experience on a daily, you can thoroughly equate that to accountability in school and discipline. So when I'm trying to break down the school-to-prison pipeline for somebody, I literally ask them these questions. "When you're driving, what do you get?" Nervous. "Somebody pulls you over. What do you get then?"

MOORE: Nervous.

CAMPBELL-GOOCH: Right. Somebody else pulls you over, what do you get then?

MOORE: More nervous.

CAMPBELL-GOOCH: Okay, so do they give you a ticket? If you keep getting pulled over for speeding, they're gonna give you a ticket, right?

MOORE: Yeah.

CAMPBELL-GOOCH: Yeah, so you keep getting tickets. What's going to happen?

MOORE: You're gonna get your license suspended.

CAMPBELL-GOOCH: Right. And if you get caught driving without a license, what's going to happen?

MOORE: You're gonna get put in jail.

CAMPBELL-GOOCH: Exactly, right. And if you keep going to jail, what happens next?

MOORE: You stay in jail.

CAMPBELL-GOOCH: Right, and then you go to prison. If you come out of prison, what you on?

MOORE: You can't get housing. You not driving, lack of employment opportunities.

CAMPBELL-GOOCH: Right, because you're on probation or parole. That system exists in our schools. You keep showing up to class late. You get a referral or demerit depending on where you are. You keep getting referrals, you get put in ISS, which really looks very similar to solitary confinement. You keep going to in-school suspension, you go to out-of-school suspension. You come back from out-of-school suspension.

MOORE: You're behind.

CAMPBELL-GOOCH: My students will say, "I'm on papers," which is ironically very similar to what somebody will say on parole. We've trained our students to experience these punitive forms of accountability and not get any of their needs taken care of. Like you said, they're behind, just like once you come out of prison you're behind, because you were frozen in time when you went in. But what I'm really hoping, and I think where we're at in Nashville . . . and this is one of my hopes . . . it feels like people are more understanding that that system of punitive punishment when it comes to accountability is not the way you actually change people. The way you change people is giving them an opportunity to restore by centering the harm.

MOORE: How did you get into activism and social justice work in general? Where did the inspiration come from?

CAMPBELL-GOOCH: My mom is the first Black General Sessions [court] secretary. So I was able to see behind the curtain. She got that job in '88 and I was born in '89. I even tell her like, all that frustration that she felt, all that hostility toward the people around her, all that lack of control, was just pushed out right to me. So being somebody who grew up down there, it used to be judges that would babysit me behind closed doors in the courtroom. I saw how the system just doesn't hold Black lives as precious. Really gave me an upbringing where I'm like, "Aw yeah. We got to figure this out."

There's also something very interesting that I read not too long ago, I think it's by Cedric J. Robinson. The book might even been called like *Black Marxism: The Making of the Black Radical Tradition*, and he posed it like, it's Black folks' proximity to whiteness that activates them. Because some of our folks don't ever see how much is being stolen. Who don't ever get to see behind that curtain. They only working to survive. But it's the ones who actually see and get close that's like, "Y'all got everything here that we would need to solve a problem there. But y'all don't want to give it to us." So we need to organize, to take it, and that's where I am with it.

I got pulled over twenty-eight times. The majority of the men in my family were swept up in a RICO case at one point in time. Also, I had classmates that were gunned down. I grew up in 37208, which is known to have the highest levels of incarceration. If you drill down even further in that, they have the highest levels of incarceration for people born in the eighties. So these are my friends, my neighbors, the people I went to kindergarten with. In the zip code that we were in, we were more likely to go to prison than anywhere else.

Highlight Nashville very specifically. In Davidson County the livable wage is $51,000. So you have to have a salary of $51,000 in order to survive here. But the average person in North Nashville makes $19k, and the average two-parent households make $21k. In that gap is all the social ills that we see every single day. But what if I was to tell you there's programs out here that fix that gap? We talk about universal basic income, guaranteed basic income, direct cash transfers. Even when we talk about accountability, we talk about violence interruption. But it almost feels like the knowledge about these things is being intentionally held back so we can't solve the problem.

MOORE: What would you say to the Black folks that maybe just believe, "Every four years I cast my vote, that's more comfortable for me to do"?

CAMPBELL-GOOCH: What I would say back is, "What are you voting for?" That would be my question. If that question is stumping you, it's because we haven't built an agenda. So the thing that we're missing in Nashville for Black folks is a shared community vision. If we get a shared community vision, we've already done. Okay, I'm going to get real heady.

MOORE: Okay, let's go. Let's get it.

CAMPBELL-GOOCH: Very basic civic engagement shit. Nashville's local government is what we call a mayor-dominant system. So, if you had a flow chart in front of you, it would say *mayor* at the top. Of course, it should say *voters* at the top, but we know that there is some other shit. Then every single branch, anything that has anything to do with our tax dollars is going to come directly from the mayor. The mayor can make a decision and then they could change anything here. We also have the second largest city council in the country. That's second to Chicago. So we have a lot of city council members. It takes half plus one to get anything moved in city council. So, look at it like this—and this is a broad stroke so I'll lose a lot of context in this—the mayor makes a decision, council controls the purse. If you don't have an agenda, or you don't have a shared community vision, it is very difficult to move anything through that structure. You have a lot of different people that you need to move at one time.

So when we talk about community and politics, we are going to have to start working to merge them. Because our existence as a community is political already. The thing that we can agree on is that all of these systems were built to maintain and control Black bodies. So in order to change that, we're going to have to build out something new and then hold them accountable to making sure our demands are met. That's why one thing that I'm really excited for next year is we've been holding these Black autonomous spaces called the Black Nashville Assembly, that's a call out to anyone who identifies on the spectrum of Blackness, all the way from African American, Afro-Latinx, Afro-Caribbean, and making sure that we can do three things: One, build a collective analysis—what are our issues as Black folks in Nashville? Two, build collective solutions—what do we want to do to solve these issues? So, if you identify poverty is one of those issues, we could talk about guaranteed basic income and how that is used globally. Then three—what's the collective action? Once we build those three things out, then we can actually build out a political agenda, and we can start voting our actual services, we can start voting our actual needs, and not just who appears to be more popular. We're changing from that, because we have very rigid ideas that we need to move. For each city council member you really only need three hundred folks in a district in order to flip the seat. And if we talk about movements in general, we know that it was only 2 percent of Black churches that participated in anything Martin Luther King had going on. So, you really only need two hundred dedicated Black folks in Nashville to change anything. Because it's going to be early adopters and later adopters. You get two hundred early adopters, you can pretty much change the world.

MOORE: What do you see allies' roles being best suited to for Black folks moving forward?

CAMPBELL-GOOCH: That's a difficult question. I was having this conversation with the homie the other day, and the homie was just, "I rocks with some of y'all." He was like, "I rocks with some of the white folks, especially the ones that's at Thanksgiving disowning they racist grandfather, causing all kinds of hell at the family dinner." And so you have two roles. You're either going to build or destroy. Sometimes you got to destroy to build. So I think we need to really talk about how we have harmed people at an epigenetic level, multi-generation. And it's going to take twice as long to get out of it than it did to get into it. So for allies, for co-conspirators, I know that there's going to be a need to jump into it headfirst and take way too much room. Those folks need to do self-work.

Whiteness, white supremacy has corrupted everything, and until everyone is willing to accept that it has corrupted everyone and that it is constantly socializing everyone to behave in a way that is actually counter-conducive to Black folks, then we are never going to move forward.

Scan the QR code to watch
the interview with Jamel
Campbell-Gooch on YouTube.

CHAPTER TWO

JOSHUA BLACK

There are many examples of entertainers using their art to take on social justice issues. Art is a unique universal language that gives voice to individuals and communities and is accessible across social boundaries. Josh Black, stand-up comedian and artist, is a recent example of how people can intentionally use their talents to raise awareness and engage the problems of our time.

Born and raised in North Nashville, Josh details his journey into comedy but also his internal growth into who he is as a person and how being from North Nashville impacted that growth.

When taking a social justice approach to entertainment, you will push some folks away, but that was a risk Josh was willing to take, and it has paid off. He is a regular at Zanies Comedy Club and is frequently featured in the *Nashville Scene*. Josh has become a local celebrity and viral sensation. His standup act is riveting and his social media videos highlighting life in Tennessee have reached hundreds of thousands of views.

Should more of our local celebrities take a responsibility to address social issues and share their perspectives? If so, how would this change how we support or don't support our artist and entertainers?

MOORE: Let's talk about the evolution from Lip to Sir Josh Black. How did that happen for you? Because I know it didn't just happen.

BLACK: Well, I would say first, being in North Nashville . . . it's so much Black business, three HBCUs in one part of town, so much culture there. I think it told us *Black pride*, just on the subconscious level. Alkebu-Lan right here, the parade on Jefferson Street is just pride. So you're proud to be Black, as opposed to going to maybe in the suburbs, or growing up in West Nashville. It's not the same. North Nashville is just so Black. Then I went to a few Black private schools. I got kicked out of probably about twelve schools. I wasn't even a fighter. Most people think you was fighting. No. I was just doing crazy shit. I put a tack in a teacher's chair.

So I went to a few Black private schools. They were teaching us civil rights shit early. Like third grade, learning about the sit-ins and all this shit. I started hating bullies, too, naturally. Bullies be picking on somebody who don't want no smoke and I hate that, I hate it, you know, how they treated people in the Civil Rights Movement. So that was just naturally kind of already in me. And then as you get a little older you start seeing stuff. So I start reading a few different things. I went to college, but I didn't give a shit about learning. They just told you, "Go to college, that's what you do." You, eighteen, I need you to pick what you want to do for the next seventy years. Like, bruh, I don't fucking know. So I'm in that thing smoking, chilling, trying to find girls.

All that to say, ironically, once I left college I started learning to love to read a little bit. I'm like damn, this is lit. The first one I read, I really hate to sound like a prison n****, was *48 Laws of Power* and I was like, "Oh shit." It was so much shit in there about how white people move. And just how the game is. I learned so much from that. So I kept moving, kept moving, kept learning shit, and then boom, started rapping. I was in my bag rapping.

MOORE: He was in his bag rapping.

BLACK: I really was. I was taking this serious.

MOORE: Did you have braids or locks then?

BLACK: I was locked up. I had locks down to my chest and I was rapping it out and that taught me how to observe something, write it down, then communicate it on a record. I did that for like four or five years. Just rapping, rapping, rapping. Just couldn't catch no break. So then finally, I got a job. It was like, a serious job with benefits and I was like, "Man, they talk about, if I do something like that, they might fire me.

If I say some shit in raps." How can I express myself but at the same time not get jammed up with that?

So I went to a comedy night, open mic. I tried it. It went off. I've been doing that shit ever since. So then I start cooking up to that. So now I got to find the name, because you know first I'm Josh Lipscomb. That's my government name. When I started reading I was like, "Man, Lipscomb school is here and the reality is they got their money off slavery and they passed a name to my family, and that's how I'm Josh Lipscomb." And I'm like, "I'm not going to be out here grinding with that name on my back." It felt like it was a stab in the back. I was Geno Griffin when I was rapping. Okay, then I switched it up because Griffin is a white name too. That ain't gonna get it. I can't do that. So then I was Muslim for a minute. So I was Josh Ali. Then I wasn't Muslim no more, that's not going to work. So then I went real crazy. This is the stupidest name ever came.

MOORE: But this is the process of you finding out who you are.

BLACK: Luckily I didn't pop with one of the names, because if I would have popped I would have been Josh Ali to this day and I'm not even Muslim. So then I went super Black. I went insane. I start googling African names. Now, my name is Mansa Rashidi doing comedy. I'm doing comedy and they like next up we have Mansa Rashidi and I said n****s in the hood gonna kill me. People in general from the city, who know me, they would never call me that. Like, they're never going to accept. So finally, I just said, "Man, I love Blackness. I love myself. I can just rep Blackness. Just Josh Black." That worked, it stuck. It didn't seem too extra. So now I'm Josh Black, doing comedy.

I'm doing stand-up every night and every night I'm like, "Man, I want to do Zanies." That's the biggest stage in the city. Zanies was like, yeah, we good. We don't know. I was like, bet. I didn't take it personal. I didn't like it, but didn't take it personal. Now I'm grinding it out, grinding it out. I'll throw my own shows then. If you're gonna let me, I'm not gonna wait on you. So now I'm throwing my own shows, getting a popping. I got seventy people coming and I don't even have a name. Then I got eighty people coming. I learned how to use social media to market it. I do a cool video, promote it on Facebook, $50, and seventy people out, so now I'm in there. I'm charging $10 a head. So I get some back.

So I go to Atlanta with it. I'll bring like one hundred people out in Atlanta. I said, "Aw hell, it's over with." So what I'm going to do is do Atlanta, Chat, Memphis, I'm finna do Charlotte. So I booked Charlotte and Charlotte said, "You can do it next month." As soon as I'm about to go out there COVID hit, bam. Shut down everything. No shows. All my contacts, all the momentum, gone. And, you know, it looks like comedy's just done. It was all so uncertain. When it first hit we were like, "You're never going to church again. You're never going to the store. All that congregating shit, it's over." I was like, fuck!

So I just sat there. First, I was like, "Fuck it. I guess I can't do comedy no more." It looked like it would never come back. And then I said, "Man, let me just try to do some videos." So I was on Twitter one day and somebody said, "Is Madison out East?" and everybody was talking about it. I'm like, "Man, they stupid as hell. Let me do a video about this shit," and I did it, and that motherfucker did like four thousand views. I'm like "four thousand, alright." So I hit him again. I said, "Let's do Antioch, I'll talk about Antioch." That shit got about ten thousand. I said "Shit let me do out North." Twenty.

So I'm lit. I'm still like, "Damn, I still got this little pocket." Like it's only Black people in Nashville that fuck with me. I'm like, it's a little small pocket, but I'm just going to eat it up. So then I said, man, I can talk to them white folk too, so let me do East Nashville. That way, I can mix it up. So now I'm doing the new East Nashville and I did that one. It was over with. Like I was scared. I'm like, "Man, if I do this shit n****s gonna be like, man, this n**** sold out." Or white might be offended because Imma keep it a thousand. But I was like, I just gotta do it. And luckily that motherfucker hit on point and everybody fucked with it. After that, it was like, it's over.

I made a conscious decision to talk to certain people. So you know, you can't please everybody. So I told myself the conservatives and the Trumpys, fuck you. It's just what it is. You can watch, but I'm making a conscious decision to say fuck y'all, I'm not talking to y'all. I'm not trying to grab y'all. It is what it is. I'm not going to convince you, sway you. I'm talking to Black people, Black allies, that's it. And once I did that, they ate it up.

MOORE: Unfortunately, I think that's a mental battle all Black folks go through at some point in time. Do I conform and play this system? Many of us do, because that's where the money is and we're conditioned to do that. Some people say, "Nah, I'm gonna take the stairs instead of the elevator," which takes a little longer, but you get to the top and you in shape and you ready for war.

BLACK: And you keep your integrity.

MOORE: And yourself, and nobody can take that away from you. And when people speak to you and look into your eyes, they're like, "Okay, I can't offer him or her a particular amount of money to do something or not do something."

BLACK: If you're white and you're an ally to Black people, if I say Jesus was Black, that doesn't offend you. You'd be like, "Yeah, facts." That's like somebody white saying "we invented the internet" and I get mad at it. It's facts. It is what it is. But the conservatives and all the racist whites, they're not going to like it. So I'm like, "You know what, fuck you."
Another reason I think it worked is because nobody talks to Nashville, especially Black Nashville. We got the white Nashville. But Memphis gets respect. So when I started talking specifically right at Nashville, I think people were like, "What the fuck is this shit?" We never heard talk about Paul's Market, or Buchanan, or shit like that.

MOORE: I'm just curious man, because you're new to a lot of people, and I'm curious on that transition for you, on remaining Lip in your core but also how do you think you're perceived?

BLACK: I don't know. I like it a lot. I'm not gonna lie. Because now, it went from like nothingness and doing the same type of videos and getting fifty views, to now everywhere I go in the city somebody saying, "What's good, I love your shit, can I get a picture?" and that shit feels good. Even when I'm like, I don't want to talk to nobody, somebody walk up to me. I still love that shit. Some people don't, but my personality, I fuck with that. And it's also like, I'm doing something, and then it's weird because a lot of times they'll say thank you, which is crazy for a comedian, like "What?" "Thank you for what you're saying to the community." I'm like, fuck. So it gives me a little purpose and I don't want to lean into it too deep. I mean you people don't know me, so I don't want to act like it's real genuine love, because you know how that shit flip on you, but it does feel good to be rewarded for hard work.

MOORE: How do you feel about Nashville now?

BLACK: Well, change is inevitable, one. So nothing in life can stay the same, nothing. So it's inevitable, and it's awkward. And there's good and bad to everything. With this new change, it is insane because it's like, "Whoa, our whole life, our grandmama, their whole life, is in North Nashville, and now it's changing and it's almost like are they going to do their whitewashing, sweeping away our whole history. Are they gonna get rid of not only us, and throw us in Antioch, but are they going to get rid of what we built?"

So there's that, but then there's also another piece. The yin and yang, and two things can exist, we can be good and bad. A lot of more millennials are moving here. There's a lot more energy here because at first, we being honest, growing up it was kind of boring. But there's an energy here and these motherfuckers got money to spend, they have ideas. We can take advantage of the chain because we're in an IT city now. There's money circulating. There's moves to be made, people to meet. I throw my show, it's a lot of people coming. A good 70, 60 percent of them aren't even from here. And also we know we're at war, so when you at war it's ugly out. I mean when you at war, it's war. However, imagine being super gentrified but then you also like, in North Dakota. Not only are you gentrified, but ain't shit going on either.

It's fun here, which I like I said, it's something. Huskies weekend . . . there's an energy. That's a Black Renaissance, Black art community's going crazy. We got Gideon's Army going crazy. And who knows? Maybe if we weren't at war so hard, and the police wasn't so racist, we might not even have a Gideon's Army most likely. That's a reaction to the police. So, we got Gideon's Army, we got Black Lives Matter Nashville, so we out here. Luckily, we have a community that's woken up to help teach us and help push us.

Nashville's in a very good spot. I think we're in a place across this country where like, Black folks in particular are in unique positions to lead us out and actually change the material conditions for our folks. So I'm excited.

Scan the QR code to watch
the interview with Joshua
Black on YouTube.

PART II

LIFE IN PRISON

CHAPTER THREE

THEEDA MURPHY

If we abolished police, jails, and prisons as they are today in the United States, how would you feel? Why would you feel that way?

Theeda Murphy is an activist, counselor, and abolitionist. She was born in Chicago in the sixties and her earliest memories are of rallies, marches, and community advocacy. She is a proud product of Oakwood University and Fisk University, both HBCUs.

Theeda's experiences working as a crisis counselor in community mental health has given her a deep understanding of the mental health delivery system and the unsung heroes who are dedicated to helping the most vulnerable in our society. She is currently working as one of the co-directors for No Exceptions Prison Collective, where she uses all of her knowledge and skills toward abolishing the carceral state and healing the harm it has caused.

It may be hard for many people to imagine a society without jails, prisons, and police, but it is not for her. Theeda takes us to a place where we all must ask ourselves, as Americans, Are we in love with harm and punishment?

As you read this conversation on abolition, reflect on whether you may be for it or against it and why you feel that way. Policing, jail, and prison have not stopped crime from growing in the United States. Is it time we try something different? What does that look like?

MOORE: I'm really excited about this conversation because you've been doing this work fighting for justice for a long time. So I want to start at the beginning. What inspired you to get into the work that you're currently doing?

MURPHY: I feel like I was born into it. My mama was a hell of a woman and she is definitely the reason I am the way I am today. I was born in Chicago and she used to take me to Operation PUSH [People United to Serve Humanity] meetings.[1] We went out and I witnessed. Those are my earliest memories, so I have no choice but to be what I am, right now.

MOORE: What impact did Fisk University have on your life?

MURPHY: I learned a lot about race relations because back in the late nineties it was probably the only place in Nashville where we could have really honest conversations about race. And we weren't afraid of repercussions, much to the chagrin of the administration at Fisk. We would talk about anything. So I got a chance to really, really see how the politics of power work and racial dynamics in those situations. I really started honing my own political framework. I would say the Race Relations Institute with Dr. Winbush as director was definitely Black nationalist and Pan-Africanist. So we were pushing reparations. Those are the type of things that really shape me.

MOORE: How did this start affecting your career path?

MURPHY: My choice of religious expression was definitely political because, you know, I feel like almost everything I do as a Black woman is political. So if I am choosing to live my full life and be my full self as a political decision, I'm going for it. Y'all go have opinions about how I live my life and what I do so, you know, fuck it. Live life the way I want to live it.

MOORE: Right, right. I believe everybody that has this type of mentality comes to understand that professionally there are consequences and repercussions.

MURPHY: I switched careers from the corporate accounting career to working in community mental health. My first job was with the police department, which was not as much of a problem as you would think, because at the time the person who was over Behavioral Health was Dr. Lorraine Greene. Dr. Greene is no longer with us. She was a revolutionary. And so being in that department with her, I learned so much. I did not have a problem with her. She had a problem with the rest of the department but any hits that came, she took those hits. I didn't have to take them, right, and I appreciated that and I respected her for what she was attempting to do in the police department. If anybody could do that type of counseling or community work in the police department it would have been her, but it wasn't working, which showed me that that is not the place for that type of work. The police should not be involved in any type of mental health. I learned that watching her try to make it work and getting all the pushback that she got.

MOORE: There's a program out there right now, where the mental health advocates and police are working together here in Nashville.

MURPHY: What most people don't know about that program is that they are already counselors within the police department. When I was there in the early nineties, they were already trying to reform the police by bringing in mental health and it didn't do shit. It didn't change anything about the culture. It didn't help. We were very limited in what we could do for people. And the reason that is, is because everything we did was mediated by police department culture. It was mediated by a police department. So they would determine who was worthy of treatment. And that should never be. That should not be something that's gate kept by them. That's why it didn't work.

MOORE: Why do you feel that, as a nation and even here in Nashville, there seems to be an agenda to have police involved in everything?

MURPHY: Money! If you remember, pre-pandemic, 2019, when we were talking about the police department and mental health, their line was "we're not social workers, we shouldn't be expected to do that." And so those of us who were pushing to divest, otherwise known as defund the police—a term that I do not like—we were saying, "okay, then let's invest in mental health." Then it became very clear that when we said "invest in mental health," we meant money. They're not giving up any money. So now they want to be social workers because they don't want to give up the money. That's all it is. They would do anything to keep their budget from being cut.

Their answer to this so far has been to build a whole hospital, but it's in the jail. And they come up with all these lovely little specialty courts. You can be diverted to treatment, but you got to get arrested first. And now they're talking about building this big juvenile jail. Instead of just building a center in the community where the kids are not involved with the courts, where police are not involved, instead of doing that and where the threat of incarceration is not hanging over everyone.

MOORE: Why don't you like the phrase defund the police?

MURPHY: Because I'm an abolitionist.

MOORE: So just get rid of them?

MURPHY: Fuck them.

MOORE: I think that more people want police than don't want police.

MURPHY: I know. I know that not very many people are abolitionist with me.

MOORE: I'm not sure if I'm an abolitionist. I know something needs to change. If we don't have police, what do we have?

MURPHY: That's the hang up. Because we know what we have now ain't working, but we don't have anything else in place. So I take it seriously that our job as abolitionists is to start building those alternative structures and to show people that they do work.

MOORE: Are there other programs that are in pilot phases in other parts of the city or the world where communities are experimenting with it? What if we don't have police in this traditional way involved in our community?

MURPHY: Yeah, there are other abolitionists in other cities who are grappling with this problem. Mainly where it has been coalescing is around mental health and I think mainly because that's the easiest thing to conceptualize. Because it's easy to for people to say, "Yeah police shouldn't be involved in the mental health crisis."

MOORE: I want to go back to talk a little bit about the organization that you are co-director of, No Exceptions Prison Collective, collaborating toward abolition and liberation. Tell us a little bit more about what the organization does and its mission.

MURPHY: We are abolitionists in every sense of the word. So yes, we are trying to abolish the prison industrial complex. We don't feel like cops and cages need to exist, but we are also slavery abolitionists, because slavery still exists. The Thirteenth Amendment has that big exception, that huge exception. We want no exceptions. That exception has been doing so much work, which is why we have the biggest prison population that has ever existed in all of history. Because of that exception. And those people are slaves.

MOORE: So one might ask: If we abolish prisons, jails, these cages that people are put in, how's that managed when a community member is harmed by another community member?

MURPHY: Right, so the idea of abolition, in order for it to work, society has to change completely and at a very fundamental level. We have to not just ask ourselves about how long people should be in jail. We have to ask ourselves as a society why are we producing so many people that we have to put away. The answers to that are that we have so many people who live in communities that are under-resourced, people who don't have health care, people who don't have places to stay, people who don't have food, people who don't have jobs that allow them to live. That's what we begin with in abolition. We begin with that. So what we're talking about is nothing less than a wholesale change in how we deal pretty much with everything in this society. One of the things that really bothers me, when I deal with Americans in particular, is this American urge to punish people. We enjoy watching people suffer and get what they deserve, and that gets in the way of developing systems that don't have punishment at their center, because if you think about it, all of our institutions, including the institutions that are supposed to be helpful, all have punishment and coercion at their core. They're all punitive.

MOORE: And we learn it, right? If you do end up going to jail or prison, you've already been trained.

MURPHY: Yes, because all of our institutions are just different flavors of prison, all of them.

MOORE: So get rid of everything, tear everything down, and start addressing the things that are putting people in those situations that end up in a courtroom.

MURPHY: Yes, yes. Because the whole idea of putting someone away for a certain amount of time is not addressing what happened. It is absolutely not addressing what happened. Transformative justice, restorative justice tries to get at what happened between these people that led to this harm, and what can we do to address it? What can we do to keep it from happening again? I believe the more we try to do that, we strengthen relationships between people. We allow people to grow beyond the mistakes they made and the harm they caused and remain in community. Then we don't end up destroying people and communities in the name of public safety.

NOTE

1. Operation PUSH, founded by Jesse Jackson, was an organization that advocated Black self-help and achieved a broad audience for its liberal stances on social justice and civil rights.

Scan the QR code to watch
the interview with Theeda
Murphy on YouTube.

CHAPTER FOUR

CALVIN "FRIDGE" BRYANT

Black Americans are incarcerated in state prisons across the country at nearly five times the rate of whites. There are many historical reasons we could point to for explanation, but the primary root cause is systemic racism in laws and policy.

In 2009, Calvin Bryant was convicted of selling drugs and sentenced to seventeen years in Tennessee state prison. He was a first-time offender and could have served less than three years. Calvin served ten years. He dreamt that one day post-release he would be able to impact the lives of others.

As Calvin takes us through his journey as a star football player, former gang member, and now youth mentor, we learn about the full accountability Calvin takes for the actions that lead him to prison, but also how outdated and discriminatory drug-free school zone laws played a major role in how he was sentenced.

This led to Calvin fighting both on the inside of prison and the outside to change policy and prevent youth from making the same mistakes he did through his nonprofit Positive Inner City Kids (PICK).

MOORE: I know where you grew up, but they might not know where you grew up. So what part of Nashville are you from?

BRYANT: I'm from the south side part of Nashville, Edgehill to be exact. Twelfth Avenue South. I was there from the day I was born till I was twenty-two years old, before I went to prison.

MOORE: So how was it growing up in the Edgehill housing projects?

BRYANT: We felt like the whole world revolved around Edgehill. So, you know, growing up, we had it a little rough but we were alright, you feel what I'm saying? The love made sure we were straight. I grew up in a two-parent household. I didn't have no excuses for some of the things I've done. I was blessed with two great parents, two sisters, family surrounding me. So I grew up pretty straight.

MOORE: So growing up in Nashville, I can remember gangs. It was always sides, right? It was always North side, East side, South side, West side. East be balling, South be balling. You got to be real Nashville to know about that. It's different now . . . it looks completely different than what we grew up with. What were some of your best times?

BRYANT: Some of my best times, and funniest times, were my teenage years, you know? Going to Hillsboro High School, like you said, being a part of those rap battles that took place between East and South. We were like rivals with East Nashville. They didn't really care for us, we didn't really care for them.

MOORE: Who won the battles though?

BRYANT: South Nashville every time. South. We had a rap group called Bezzeled Gang, it's still around today, Lil Vac, PSG, Cali. And then we did our football thing. We were one of the top teams in the state.

MOORE: I saw an Instagram post of you just kind of breaking it down, like look, "I had letters from, offers from here, offers from all these big SEC schools . . ." How was that feeling, getting all of those offer letters to all of these top D1 schools?

BRYANT: It was something new to me, and also to the neighborhood. When we became the powerhouse football program at Hillsboro, what was surprising is the talent that we had. We never had that before. So we start getting offers from Tennessee, Michigan, Auburn, Oregon. All the SEC schools were interested in us. The Oregons, the Colorados, and for an inner-city kid that was big. But I think one of the things that kind of hurt me was there was no one in front of me to kind of let me know how to take that process. We end up not having great ACT scores, and waited too late to take them, and we didn't take our recruiting trips the way we were supposed to. You could be the most highly recruited player ever, but if you don't have your grades together and your mind right to step up to that business part of it, you're just another person that could have went somewhere.

MOORE: I think all of us, especially when we were the first ones to be exposed to something new, we have nobody to help us navigate those situations. So we kind of try to figure it out as we going. And you know, seventeen years old, we're looking for an adult to tell me how to do this. That's real important to mention, but also it's important for people like yourself to do what you're doing now, going back and making sure kids know how to navigate those systems. Because now you see, now like you got social media and a little more resources, but it wasn't like that when you were coming up.

So you end up going to TSU, Tennessee State University. How was that experience?

BRYANT: You know, it was a bunch of ups and downs. People that know me best, they know that I wasn't supposed to go to Tennessee State University. I broke my ankle in the game before the state championships, so I lost a lot of big colleges that recruited me, but the love Tennessee State showed me . . . They had Coach Reese there at the time. They had Ms. Teresa Phillips as the athletic director. And one night man, I'm laying up at home in the Edgehill projects, and we heard a knock on the door. My leg was broke and in walked the whole Tennessee State coaching staff. It was probably like seven, eight o'clock in the evening. And you know, it just really touched me in a way. Like I'm a kid sitting here with a broken ankle. Not too much I can do for anybody's university right now, and they gave me a full scholarship offer. I signed that night. Let them know that, yeah, I was committed to that.

So when I got up to Tennessee State University the year after I got there I had to get my grades right through Prop 48. That was a kind of academics thing. And Coach Reese was fired, bro. So they brought in another coach by the name of James Webster. He wasn't feeling me the way Coach Reese was, you know, he felt like I should earn this and that. But we end up having a down season, which was like two wins nine losses. He took my scholarship. A lot of people don't know that. So he took my scholarship, we kind of had words because I'm looking at it like "I'm an inner city kid on a full scholarship. It's not my fault, what happened to us. But you took my scholarship and I got to pay to go to school." I'm not going to pay to play at Tennessee State University with the kind of talent that I had. So, you know, one thing led to another and I felt that day like I'd lost my love for the game. So I stepped away for a minute. I try to tell kids a small step can be a major factor in your life. It can end up leading to something bad.

MOORE: Let's get into that. A lot of people may be familiar with your story. Especially, you know, around school zones, drugs in school zones, and I'll preface this a little bit and let you dive in deeper. You know, you're twenty-two years old and really, if the system was to have it their way, you would technically still be in prison until 2023. You got a seventeen-year sentence for something that should have been a three-year sentence for a first-time offender. And you were the first they applied that to in Davidson County. That's crazy. First-time offender. But there's the back story on the drugs, and how you were kind of pressured by a so-called friend. Talk to me, talk us through that a little bit.

BRYANT: You know, some people are probably sitting back like, "How did this kid get this much time for nothing basically, drugs and stuff?" My decisions as a child and my leadership in the community cost me later. What I mean by that is I joined the GDs, the Folks, which was the Gangster Disciples, Growth and Development, whatever they want to call it. It wasn't them that was the problem. It was just a growing gang problem in my neighborhood. So me being a leader, that was how I was seen, with coward-ass dudes getting into positions where they were making calls, I feel like it was the best decision for me and my family to get involved and change it from the inside out. Well, I'm just a fifteen-year-old kid at the time. By the time I'm sixteen, I got the attention of the whole city, not for negative things, but for being a football star already.

But negative news travels faster than positive news. When everybody found out I was a part of this organization, that was like a big story, even though we weren't doing anything wrong. So after I got done playing football and I'm at TSU and things like that, the police department get ahold to like, "This guy's a high-ranking gang member."

So to kind of fast forward, when I was in the projects this guy wore a wire on me three times. And when we say *pressure* and *peer pressure*, peer pressure doesn't have to be someone trying to beat you up if you don't do it. It could just be constantly bringing it up. So basically what he told me was like, "Look man, I got a white boy that want some pills." So I didn't think nothing of it. I said I got a homeboy who be having pills. I didn't follow up on it. But he kept coming back to me. "What's up?" So I gave him twenty pills the first time. One hundred pills the second time. Two hundred pills the third time. On sealed indictments when they build a case on you, I might deal to you today, I might do one tomorrow, one next month. But all that's going to be on one case. They're intentionally making your case look worse.

So the whole time he was wired up on me in the middle of the projects. He had caught a driving charge. They said they were trying to clean up the Edgehill area, for whatever reason, and asked if he knew me. So he was like, "Yeah I know Fridge." So the investigation started, he wore a wire on me, I end up getting arrested on May 16, 2008. Sealed indictments, three transactions, with this law called the Drug Free Schools. My bond was like $350,000. So everyone was like, "What the fuck is a drug-free school zone?" Nobody knew. I didn't know, so I'm thinking, "I'll be back home like the rest of these dudes."

But what I didn't know was in 1995 they passed a law for people standing on school grounds serving drugs. So the district attorney's office at that time was manipulating the law. All they wanted was to know something about GD. I couldn't tell nothing about GD. So since

I wanted to be a tough guy, so called, they hit me with the drug-free school zone. So we're going to sentence like, "You're a gang leader, whether we can prove it or not." It's any sale or delivery that takes place within a thousand feet of a daycare, school, library, community center. So anywhere in the inner city or projects you're going to be in a school zone. But they never applied it to people until it came to me.

When I went to trial the first time, a dude from my neighborhood got on the stand against me. We had a hung jury. The jury was like, "He's no better than Fridge." So this is how slick the prosecutors were. The next trial they took him off the act, like they couldn't find him. They put a detective on the stand and read his testimony like he was him, which is illegal. We've got the right to cross-examine a witness or whoever it is. They found me guilty and sentenced me to seventeen years at 100 [percent].

The only two charges that you can get 100 percent on have something to do with kids. Compare a child molester to a guy selling drugs in a drug-free schools zone. Keep in mind, my drugs were sold at 10:00 and 6:00 at night. No kids around. The schools are closed but the law was so messed up that they can still charge you whether the school was open or not.

They eventually changed the law, but I went to Charles Bass Correctional Facility. Ended up being shipped to Northwest Correctional Facility. Northwest was the worst penitentiary in the state of Tennessee. That's why I tell people, like, "They threw me to the wolves, but I came out leading the pack." When God is for you, you're going to be alright regardless where you go.

MOORE: What were some of the hard lessons you had to learn about like street life, loyalty, and what really matters during your time in prison?

BRYANT: What really hit me, man, my dad was like the dad of the neighborhood. But he was a dude that grew up in the streets, but he played football for Tennessee State, tried out for the Dallas Cowboys. A real family man. He was real all the way around and my dad never told me nothing wrong. And one day, when we were sitting there at visitation, after I went to jail for the first time, and he was telling me how, man, he was proud of me and how they were railroading me and you know, "Just keep manning up to your situation." So he asked me something and it really hit me and stuck with me. He said, "Man, you GD right?" I was like, "Yeah I am." He never asked me nothing about that, but he wasn't picking on GD. Just telling me about people in general. He said, "Your bond, I got it lowered." It was like $200,000 at the time. He says, "$20,000 will get you out of jail, right?" This how he talking to me. I said, "Yeah." He said "Look at all them GDs around you. Look at all them dudes in the neighborhood you save every day. Look at all these dudes around the city say they love you. Twenty thousand dollars isn't a lot of money."

It made me think, "Damn, man. We sacrifice so much and put our life on the line for brothers every day." Maybe you only got a handful of people that stick by you. I had real homeboys to stick by me. But it was a handful, and most of them weren't affiliated with nothing I had going on. The ones that needed me to steal called me from the penitentiary. That's cowards. They weren't there for me. I just had to boss up in my situation and know I got to do this time and come home. I got the right to live a life. For these dudes, these young dudes out here shooting and robbing with him, they're not going to be the dudes that go visit your mama, or going to be the dudes that go take care of your daughter. They're going to wear your shirt for a little while, shout you out on Instagram and shout you out on Facebook, but you'll do that thirty years by yourself.

And then it's like, look, let's be real. These dudes cooperate with the government, or the state. What are y'all gonna do, kill them? That's why it was big for me not to let none of our partners do nothing to the guy who just told on me. I'll kill him in another way. He's all through my book. The paperwork and everything. So I am not worried about putting my hands on him and killing him, because that's what they want you to do.

A lot of people not involved in criminal activity or been involved in a case don't know this. In the state of Tennessee they don't have to reveal your witness to you until ten days before trial. So a lot of times when people are going around talking about who snitched on them, they don't have the paperwork to show it. The state's intention is to reveal who snitched on you. Could be your best friend. So how they did me was ten days before trial. They drop dude's name on me. Why argue when you can say, "This is a sealed statement from the state of Tennessee." When you're a confidential informant, they give out your social security number, your address, your places you work at. That person that you telling on gets all your information, bro.

This is educational because our kids don't know this. They're just thinking, "Okay I got a situation. I'm gonna go ahead and tell on a dude." But dude will have your social security number, he got this, he got that, because they reveal everything about you. Every charge you ever caught.

MOORE: Through all those situations, how did you remain Fridge and get out and do what you are doing now?

BRYANT: Basically, man, my upbringing. I tried to stay close to what my mom and pops taught me. And you know, I had to learn how to deal with people. Like, I've always been a people person, but you gotta learn how to interact with individuals who may have committed violent crimes or have different sexual orientations or like the guards fucking with you. My main motivation was to get home to my mom. She was sick. I lost my father doing time. I was incarcerated. So I was like, "I got to get home." I knew the choices I made could stop me from getting home to her.

But I won't lie, I fought in one-on-ones and it was never because of me, bro, it was always because of somebody else. And it really broke me down to the point that I was fed up. Tired of having a ride with dudes. I don't even know. This dude might be from Knoxville, Memphis, Chattanooga, and he could be in the wrong, but just because of what I signed up for I got to ride. So I got to the point when I had the position that I lead by example. I let my guys know, look, no bullshit. You doing bullshit, we busting your ass up. So, you know, everybody can't be in a position of authority and a leader like that. And I was blessed enough with those attributes to be like, "Look man, this how this is going to go, but you got to realize there's other gorillas in there, like you, right? And another gorilla might not be on no positive stuff." So you gotta play a chess match.

It's been times before we get into it with somebody. I'm in the cell before the doors pop like, "God, let me make it through this." Because I know any day a person catches me, it could be my last day. I've seen people get killed in there. I just pray. And staying grounded and being thankful. And I feel like God's leading me out of there, but it's bullshit every day. The only peaceful time in prison is when you sleep.

MOORE: Your release was a big thing, especially for the city, because that law was pretty much unconstitutional. It was entrapment, especially for Black inner-city youth. How did you feel, being able to come home?

BRYANT: First of all, I got to give a shout out to people that stood by me through that whole process, because it was a team effort, all my family and friends. My lawyers Joy Kimbrough, Daniel Horowitz. I got released on 2018 Halloween and I'll tell you that was the craziest day ever. But my lawyer came a day before and told me I was getting out tomorrow and I didn't believe it. I said, "Ain't no way." I kind of, like, got to the point I believed that I would go home one day, but it's like, "Y'all really have to show me this one right here." So when I got to that courtroom, all of those cameras were there and I really got released that day. Social media went crazy. I was on everybody's page, interviews with [channels] 2, 4, 5, 17. It was like a dream.

MOORE: Yeah, I was living in China at the time and I heard it.

BRYANT: You think I'm lying, but this city showed me so much love. I felt like Meek and Philly. And the way they stood up for me, I can be out to eat and I didn't pay for nothing for like, two, three months. I'm talking about people just, "How you doing? How you doing, sir?" There might be money in my hand. After I get done eating I would tell the waitress, "I'm ready to pay" and all. "Somebody else paid for yours." I mean that happened for two or three months, and even to this day I still get love, man. The city of Nashville showed me so much love to be labeled a gang member. And I push that to the side and nobody having no hard feelings and just accepting who I am, accepting my organization. That love I got on a football field, I'm getting double now and helping kids and running my organization. It was really like a dream come true.

MOORE: What is your PICK foundation? Positive Inner City Kids.

BRYANT: Positive Inner City Kids was a program that I started when I was incarcerated in 2015. I had this vision that I want to equip all the kids in the community with the tools to be successful and learn from my mistakes, and regardless of their address it doesn't have anything to do with the success they can have. I got it certified through the state in 2015 and in 2018 I came out running, I got blessed in 2019 or 2020 from my big guy Ramon Foster who played with the Pittsburgh Steelers. He gave me a $10,000 grant to get it started and ever since then we've been doing amazing things in the community. We mentor, we do scholarships. We're working on field trips as we speak. We are involved with the juvenile justice system, working hand-in-hand with them. So, you know, it's major things going on in the community with us and we are open to North, East, West, South. When we can use this one program to bridge the gap between North, South, East, West, Cripps, Bloods, GDs. Whatever you are, we accept you man. We just want you to do good and let every kid know you got a home away from home, but we are going to work inside the home.

MOORE: What do you want your legacy to be?

BRYANT: I want my legacy to be, "He was the individual that came out and showed people that it's okay to do the right thing and be a stand-up guy. You don't got to do bullshit to be respected." Now I'm sitting here probably one of the most respected guys in the city, and I never robbed anybody, never killed anybody. I was a football player that made a bad decision. So to let people know, look out for everybody. Everybody needs to be a family. When you let your kid go outside, you know, it's another kid, I am responsible enough to look out for them because one day, we're not going to be able to go outside. We won't be able to sit here, we're going to be in the house, or getting a little older on the porch. We got to know that we planted the right seeds. Right now some older cats looking at me like, "I'm glad Fridge is out there doing that." So, you know, just to have that accountability for everybody and these kids learning trades, living a life and I mean living it to the fullest. Because me personally, I feel like there's a trap already set for them. One thing that's going to be the same twenty years from now is somebody is going to be going to court. Somebody going to be in juvenile. Somebody going to be in prison. How can we break the cycle?

Scan the QR code to watch
the interview with Joshua
Black on YouTube.

CHAPTER FIVE

RAHIM BUFORD

A native Nashvillian, Rahim has seen and felt how poverty negatively impacts people in the criminal legal system. Arrested at age eighteen, he spent twenty-six years of his life in seven different prisons across Tennessee before being paroled in 2015.

Upon his release from prison, Rahim received a presidential scholarship to American Baptist College and worked part time as an organizer for Children's Defense Fund Nashville. In 2017, he founded Unheard Voices Outreach to raise awareness about "felonism" and to empower formerly incarcerated persons as they transition back into the civic, economic, and technological community. Rahim graduated from American Baptist College with a bachelor's degree in entrepreneurial leadership in 2019.

He managed the Nashville Community Bail Fund from 2018 to 2021, during which time he posted bond for more than 1,200 low-income Nashvillians. Rahim uses his voice to advocate for decarceration, driven to assist currently and formerly incarcerated people in their fights to be free by his desire to see transformative justice.

MOORE: I know you grew up here in Nashville. Can you tell us a little bit about what part of Nashville you grew up in and how it was compared to what you see now?

BUFORD: My upbringing is in two parts. I was born in 1971, Hubbard Hospital out South, to a single-parent mother. I'm the third born of seven total, and my early beginnings were very humble. South Nashville, Nolensville Road. In the early parts of my life there was this street that at the very bottom of it was a fruit stand. I don't know if you are familiar with the Nolensville area, at Harding Place there used to be a Harding Mall. That was on Nolensville Road, and there was the very first Lake Providence Church, real close to a street called Flora Maxwell. And so, I lived early on on the street called Providence Heights, and my granddad had built most of those houses on top of that hill. He was a World War II veteran. It seemed normal as a kid. Because what do you know as a child? Just ripping and running, hanging with my grandmother, picking wild berries, poke salad. We actually had an outhouse. We didn't even have running water. And we got our water from next door, from Miss Maggie Mae. And I used to just play around with my brothers on top of the hill.

By the time I was five, we were living in Winstead Manor, which is on Edmondson Pike. My mother had been moved into an apartment. And by that time, there were five of us. My mom working, staying with my grandmother. And then, I think in 1977 my mom met my stepdad. Then we migrated out to northeast Nashville, Parkwood area, Brick Church Pike, Ewing Lane, Dickerson Road, and Park Wood Villa. From six all the way up till eighteen, that was what you would call my hood, my stomping ground, adjacent to Golden Valley, Oak Park, Northcrest. All that was my neighborhood. Early on, you know, school was cool. I didn't do well. I thought I was dumb actually and it was because of the grades that I made. If you didn't get a good grade, a B or C, you're thinking, you know, naturally like I must not be smart. At least, that's what I thought. But of course, later on in life, I learned that I'm an auditory learner and I need to experience education before I take it in. But also, I realized later in life that the educational stimulus was not enough to move the type of brain that I had. In other words, it was boring. I was really smart. It's just that the information that was given to me didn't appeal to me.

MOORE: The methodology didn't fit your learning.

BUFORD: Yeah. And so, you know, at a very young age man I found myself into all kinds of stuff. We were poor. I didn't think we belonged to the neighborhood. It started small, you know, as my life moved into the negative. Going to the little store, stealing bubblegum, Now & Later type stuff because we aren't having things other kids had. When the Buddies, I don't know if you even remember, they cost $1.49. They make your feet feel fine. That was the kind of things that brought about a lot of shame growing up, wearing the Cougars from Pick and Pay, the Smacks jeans, not the Lee's or the Levi's, you know, other parachute pants and things like that. So those were the worst times, you know, realizing that I was poor. And the way your status works as a kid was like, you had to have these external things to be a part of your identity. And so I said, you know, I'm not going to be a nobody. So I found myself engaging in activity that I would later learn was crime.

MOORE: We're gonna get into your journey, to the meat. But this is very important because I think, you know, prison's no game. I have family members who have been in prison, in jail, and it's a distinct difference from being in the county or even being in the fed. And you did twenty-six.

BUFORD: I was caged for twenty-six years of my life.

MOORE: Can you tell us about what led to you being encaged for twenty-six years, and then your development over those twenty-six years to where you are now?

BUFORD: I can abbreviate it and just hit certain points, and if there are things that you might want to dive deeper off into, as this is a deep-dive conversation, we can do that. But fast-forwarding to growing up in my neighborhood. I had two older brothers and one of my brothers, may he rest in peace, Robert. He was the dude that made me fight. I didn't want to fight, but he made me fight because he picked on me and it just made me. In my home this corporal punishment thing existed. And as you may know, corporal punishment dates back to coastal slavery, how whips were used to control the behavior of African enslaved individuals, and using pain to control behavior. That was implemented in my home. And I know, like, a lot of parents even today think that it's okay to use these means by which to discipline, but the result for us was it made us bad to worse. The things that happened to us, we did it to other people in the neighborhood. So being groomed to be this person that I really wasn't, but influenced to be in life, it came out in different ways.

What actually caused me to end up in prison was a series of events. First of all, at a very young age, I had a pistol in my neighborhood. If you don't have a—we call them strap, stones, piece—if you didn't have those, you felt a bit vulnerable to being harmed. That's just the way it was. I can't explain why. But what happened is I remember like yesterday, me and one of my homeboys, I'm a call him C so as not to expose who he really was, we were in this stolen car and we did a burglary. Well, I remember like yesterday, we were in this stolen car. Was a Grand Prix. I'm going down Ewing Drive. I remember like yesterday, police pull behind us. I pulled behind the Dollar Store, Brick Church Pike and Ewing Drive. Jumped up out of the car. He didn't jump out. I hit the cross street, made it home. Mama waiting on me. She said, "he already told on you." Yeah, next thing you know, I'm going to juvenile. Not for two or three days. I get a juvenile sentence. What changed me was while I was at TYC, Tennessee Youth Center in Joelton, Tennessee, my grandmother died. I didn't know how to experience death because it never happened before. So it was the first time in my life that I felt pain that hit me.

MOORE: Wow. How did you feel when C snitched on you?

BUFORD: I really didn't even think about it because they put me back in a police car. So at age sixteen I experienced police brutality because they drove us to the place where we were selling the stolen items. Police took me out of the car. I had a leather jacket, Delta Force Nikes, stone-washed jeans, and a black and white Izod shirt. Police grabbed me out of the car, lifted me up, put me on the car, not the hood of the car, but the top of the car. "Tell us where it's at, tell us, where it at?" And I didn't.

He put me back in the car. What I didn't know is he's recording, and I said, "Man, you punk ass motherfucker, what you tell them folk?" So I'm telling on myself, they're recording me.

MOORE: Wow.

BUFORD: So my grandmother's dead. I get a pass to the funeral. Me and my stepbrother, we committed a robbery within that time frame. I drove all the way down Nolensville Road, at the end of Nolensville Road, away from town. That was a Kwik Sak. We were in this Cutlass Ciera that, I hate to admit this because I feel so bad, it was a stolen car. I already had it parked somewhere. Did a robbery and I remember like yesterday, it was this song. Eazy-E. I think it was "Easy Does It." And they actually went through a robbery and I'm not saying rap influences, but it influenced me. I heard those lyrics. Remember I told you I was an auditory learner. So when I hear words, I see pictures. That's how my brain works.

MOORE: So you said, "Oh, I can do this."

BUFORD: I knew I could do it, and I did it. So, as I'm leaving the place and going back up Nolensville Road, I see the cops going that way. That changed my life forever. I didn't even know that it would. I eventually get out of juvenile. I went in in February of '88. I got out in July of '88. But I got a chip on my shoulder. I'm smoking cigarettes. I'm at home now, I don't care. My stepdad stole my pistol. We got into a fight. I'm the first of my brothers to get out on my stepdad in a fight and I know I had to leave because either he was going to kill me or I was going to kill him, and my mother knew. She said, "Son, that's not the man I married." And, you know, went through a series of like, heartfelt things, because, you know, he was abusive. I've seen things and I guess I took some of that out on him, because he hit my mother.

I left home and moved in with someone I thought was a friend. A guy that I looked up to. And the reason I looked up to him because he was the first dude to manhandle my stepdad. He saw him trying to whip me in the backyard with a belt, running, chasing me. He jumped three fences, grabbed him, picked him up. I'm like, "That's my hero, that dude put it down." Taught me how to cut hair. I love this guy, man, like a big brother to me. So moved in with him. And one day, he woke me up. He said, "Youngblood. Man, you got to go back home." He said, "I can't pay the rent." He said, "I'm Chapter 13, and I'm, I'm paying child support?" I said, "What if I can get the money?" Committed a robbery, got the money, didn't have to go back home. But guess what. The thing about stuff like that is that it gets addictive in some ways. Next thing you know, we need some more money, I need to commit a robbery.

Out in Madison there used to be a Lee's Chicken. I scoped this place out, Lee's Chicken. I went to the place, went in saw some people outside. "This is a robbery." Look, I'm just here to get the money, but I shot a gun into the floor and the bullet went *boom* and it hit a man. I ran, but I had grabbed a sack. I was a juvenile, they had my prints.

MOORE: You're already in the system.

BUFORD: I'm already in the system. May the fifth, they pick me up at the car wash right across the street from Baskin Robbins on Dickinson Road, thirty police, guns drawn, you know, they arrest me. Less than a year after—I had three judge-appointed attorneys in less than a year—I was convinced to plead guilty to a life-and-twenty-year sentence.

I'm in a penitentiary at age nineteen. I got a life-and-twenty-year sentence. They sent me from Nashville to Memphis at MLRC. From MLRC they sent me to Tiptonville, at a place where youth are. I end up getting an assault charge. They shipped me to Fort Pillow, and *ship* means *transferred* because slave language is still used in prison culture, because prison culture is a derivative from chattel slavery. Black Codes, vagrancy laws, Jim Crow. All of that is connected.

Fort Pillow where they sent me was real, because I'd never been in a prison where everything was open and you could see. They're yelling, "Fresh meat," all this kind of stuff. You know, I'm scared. I'm scared to death, I'm not gonna lie. And you can see right from one cell to the next cell, and it's the same place where Nathan Bedford Forrest killed more than four hundred African American soldiers in the Union and man, it was crazy, it was crazy. But then I started studying Islam with these Muslim brothers and turns out that I could be forgiven, that's what they told me at least. I believed it. So I started studying Islam, and then it motivated me to get my GED. Ended up getting my GED at Fort Pillow. Well, they shipped me to West High [West Tennessee State Penitentiary] or transferred me to West High. Not far across the street from West High, I ended up going to Turney Center Vietnam.[1] In 1991, before you got into the visiting gallery coming from the compound, they got a picture Nathan Bedford Forrest and General Lee on the wall.

MOORE: Wow. They set the tone.

BUFORD: Man, two Black employees, everybody else white in Hickman County. Surrounded by the Duck River. No escape, and that's from '91 to 2002. I grew up in that place. There's a lot of stuff I'm taking out. Like I met my older brother in prison, Chubby, may he rest in peace, Joe. It was three of us at the same time. I had never met him. I saw him one time when I was a kid. I didn't know who they really were, but these were my older brothers, we were in prison together.

MOORE: Y'all having family reunions in prison and stuff.

BUFORD: While I was there, man, my sister was murdered. My dad died while I was there. I remember being at the casket, looking at this dude, and I'm like, you know, it's like the Tupac *Me Against the World* album where he said, "my anger would let me feel for a stranger." So I'm looking at this man in his casket. It's my dad, but I don't feel nothing.

MOORE: This is real deep dish conversation. From your time being caged up, what were some other things that maybe people are just not aware of?

BUFORD: So, you know, while I was in prison, first it was my grandmother died. Then in '95, my dad died, 2000 my sister was murdered, 2000 my granddad died. I saw thirteen people murdered in front of me. I'm talking about murdered like in the movies. The shank's in, the blood out of the neck type thing. Those are some of the worst things you experience in prison life. But the thing is that when you're removed from society, the social death of going to prison, you immediately have to adopt a survival mentality and . . . It makes you not as human as you really are meant to be. You got to get in beast mode, so you learn things about yourself. So for the kid or the young person who's thinking about doing something, it removes your humanity to a degree, just to survive. But even more if you like birthdays, if you like partying, if you like being able to wake up in the morning and not have somebody yelling in your ear—whether it's a cellmate who you don't know, you're smelling body fluids, or some officers, some guard, some warden, somebody—you really want to think twice, because for the bad choice, one bad choice . . . I made several. One bad choice can end the rest of your life, because living in a prison is really just existing. Now for me, it became a transformative experience because I really wasn't "meant" to be there. I did wrong, but had I had the right guard rails, the right structure, guidance, I never would have gone to prison, because I learned later that I have a scientist mentality. I could have been a doctor or a lawyer, you know, I could have been anything I wanted to be, but the system threw me away because they thought that I could not be redeemed. I could not change. And that was a lie.

MOORE: Can you tell us a little bit about how you took your experience being caged up and transitioning out, helping other people in your situation? The fight for social justice around felonism?

BUFORD: So that takes us back to Riverbend Maximum Security Institution, which is where I was transferred in 2002. I heard they would have college classes from Vanderbilt. I applied to those classes, and then they told me I didn't qualify because I had no previous college experience. But I thought that was dumb. So what I did was, because I was a president of an organization, New Beginnings, I would see these students and people coming in who are free world people. And I would go stare into the window.

About the third time that I did that a lady came to the window, I mean to the door, and asked me, "Young man why are you looking through that window?" I said, "Ma'am I believe I should be in that room." She said, "Can you write an essay to tell us why?" I wrote that essay in a week, gave it back to her, and then the week after that I'm in college-level graduate courses at Vanderbilt Divinity School, and that's when I came alive and I realized that higher education on the academic level had great opportunity. My voice came alive. Her name was Reverend Janet Wolf, and we're great friends to this day. Because of that experience we created this school program called SALT schools, Society for Alternative Learning and Transformation. I would meet Dr. [Forrest] Harris, who was a Vanderbilt professor as well. He gave me a scholarship to attend American Baptist College, and he said, "When you get out." The prophecy of hearing that, *when you get out . . .* something in me said, "I'm gonna. I'm gonna get out."

In 2015, after my third parole hearing, I left with fifteen credits from Lipscomb University, three credits from Ohio University. Education became my liberation.

I'm out June the twenty-fifth, 2015. Didn't waste any time. Enrolled at American Baptist College. By that January I'm out, I'm an organizer for the Children's Defense Fund Nashville team. That following year, 2017, I incorporate the Unheard Voices Outreach to give not only a voice to formally caged citizens, but also as a way to push back against felonism. And felonism is the political, the social, the economic discrimination, disadvantaging of American citizens who are convicted of a felony. It marginalizes a whole group of people.

We have millions of people all across the United States who can't vote. But what's very sad and profound, it needs to be paid attention to, is that in Tennessee 421,000 human beings, citizens, can't vote. That's enough to swing an election. That's felonism. It's not just, "I can't get a job. I can't get an apartment." It's the political tool used by those who are in power. Unheard Voices pushes back against that.

In 2018, getting ready to get into the last phase of my college experience, I needed an experience field training. I met Dawn Deaner, who was the chief public defender at the time. Elected public defender. She introduced me to the Nashville Community Bail Fund founders, because I'm trying to get some support for Unheard Voices. But I also get the opportunity to get this field training out of the way. They made me an offer I can't refuse. They said, "We will support you and Unheard Voices, but would you consider working with the Nashville Community Bail Fund?" This is in 2018, March, something happened to the bail fund manager at the time. She resigned. They asked me if I'd be willing to step up and see if I like it. I absolutely step all the way up to become the Nashville Community Bail Fund manager.

In 2019 I graduate from American Baptist College summa cum laude. Yeah, and so now I'm a college graduate. My work is decarceration. I've bailed out more than nine hundred Nashvillians from jail because of the Nashville Community Bail Fund. And what it does is it bridges the gap between those without wealth and those who have wealth, and says they should be treated the same. And so we bail people out of jail who are only charged with offenses. There's this misunderstanding about people going to jail and people thinking that they're guilty, but that's not the case. We've learned in the Nashville Community Bail Fund over 50 percent of the cases that people are charged with are not prosecuted. No one is found guilty. You see, so what does that say about the larger picture of what is happening with wealth-based detention? We're moving now to change how bail is done in Nashville on the pre-trial level. Because really just like those who are imprisoned, those who in the pre-trial level, only the poor people get the short end of the stick and end up staying there. If you got money, you don't spend the night in jail. You see what I'm saying? And so, what we learn and what I know now is that it's the general sessions judges, who appoint commissioners or magistrates, who set bail amounts. This is not TCA statute.

So any dollar amount is a ransom that you put on somebody's body, just because there is this thing that we're still addicted to, and that's putting a price tag on a poor Black body. Rooted in slavery, again, because when Black people were being freed on the plantations, some were still on the plantations, and Black people who had been freed would pull money together and buy the freedom of a loved one. Bail funds are the same principle.

Nashville Community Bail Fund will go get that person out of prison. They're not guilty. We're talking about mothers and fathers. We're talking about people who can lose their jobs. We're talking about people who can lose their children on charges that we know 50 percent of are dismissed.

MOORE: I know people want to reach out and figure out how they can help and support.

BUFORD: With the Nashville Community Bail Fund, all anyone has to do is just Google "Nashville Community Bail Fund." All the information is there. With the Unheard Voices Outreach, we also have a watcher's project where a lot of people in prison file for post-conviction. They go into these empty courtrooms alone in chains and shackles, blue jeans, white stripe, blue shirt, and get treated like they don't even matter. So we want to put eyes on this process and say, "Yes, you do matter." But even more than that, we're connected to the Choosing Justice Initiative as we move to reform indigent defense, because in Nashville, if you're poor, a judge chooses your attorney. Can you imagine that the same person who is about to announce judgment on your case is also selecting your attorney? So we want to put eyes on that process, but in addition to that, Unheard Voices Outreach has a No Vote, No Citizen, No Freedom Campaign to reach out to the 421,000 people who can't vote. We formed this community so we can empower ourselves, so we can be self-determined and finance the operations to get our voting birth rights back. In the early eighties even people in prison voted. This is a recent thing in Tennessee. A lot of people have this false belief that people can't vote because they get convicted of a felony. That's not what happened. It's the people in power, ultra-conservative Republicans in Tennessee, who said, "You know what, it's to our advantage to disadvantage all you who get these felonies that we created."

Let me say that again. They were created. What do I mean by that? Felonies are created by legislatures, the very thing that this country is built on. You took a whole country, America, all right. Five thousand African American people or more were lynched. Nobody went to prison. We got kidnapping, we got robbery, we have language, culture, religion, God taken from a whole people. And those like myself, you're saying I can't wholly fully participate in society because I made one bad choice. Yeah, I did wrong. I did twenty-six years. But here it is. All these people are doing the same things. They don't even go to prison.

I mean Daniel Hambrick, come on. Man got shot in his back seven times. The police officer got a $25,000 bail. But then you arrest this woman over here on a DUI, give her a $400,000 bail, and she died in jail recently, in the last sixty days. That's why we do this work. That's why I'm doing what I'm doing. And that's why I'm pushing back on the system. Because if you can send me to prison, and I got to do my time and I got to be held accountable, why not you?

NOTE

1. Turney Center Industrial Complex. It earned the nickname Turney Center Vietnam due to all of the deaths from gang violence.

Scan the QR code to watch
the interview with Rahim
Buford on YouTube.

PART III

THE ELECTED

CHAPTER SIX

CHRISTIANE BUGGS

A member and former chair of the Metro Nashville Public Schools Board of Education, Christiane Buggs is a Nashville native and former MNPS student. Her teaching and civil service experience runs the gamut of Nashville's public education system.

Christiane breaks down education to help us reflect on the roles we all play when it comes to making decisions around educating our communities. Whether it be public or charter or private, do we really want to create an equitable education system where all students are provided resources based on what they need to be successful?

Christiane recently became the Director of Strategic Partnerships at Tennessee Educators of Color Alliance. Before that she served as the manager of literacy partnerships for the Blueprint for Early Childhood Success, a United Way of Greater Nashville initiative focused on increasing literacy in our youngest learners.

As a student, teacher, and community member, she has experienced our schools in many different ways throughout the course of her life.

MOORE: Let's get straight into it. Education is a big deal. It affects all of our community here in Nashville. But there are harmful disparities that affect people who look like me and you, specifically here in Nashville, when it comes to suspension, expulsion, and getting into the higher achievement programs. What is going on, especially from your lens being right in the thick of things? Talk to us.

BUGGS: Okay, you better be ready for a lot of nuance, a lot of data, and then just a lot of facts. I'll give it to you. In my daytime role, I am the manager of literacy partnership with United Way. So to take us back to 2017, then mayor Barry really wanted to focus on the pre-k space. What does it look like, as soon as the child is born until they're about five or six? What does it look like to make sure that they have support? Because 30 percent of our students come into Nashville schools one full grade level behind already. What can we do to impact that? But when you really break the data down, when you look at Black or Brown boys, 80 percent of our students come into the first grade a grade level behind. What's happening in our community? We're really not resourcing students. Right? That has been blowing my mind, as I have this dual role of being on the board and really looking at strategies. You have a Black son and I have a three-year-old son. There was this nervousness because of course I'm a co-parent. How do I make sure to support him? I always have these things going on in my mind as I make decisions with the school board, because I know what our students and families are facing even before they come to us.

MOORE: I am a product of MNPS public schools like yourself. With all this data, I see what's going on. I understand. What I see is, the public school system here in Nashville is not built for my son to succeed. What would you say to a parent like myself in Nashville who sees this data? They may also be products of MNPS or public schools in different cities and states. How would you encourage them to give MPNS a chance?

BUGGS: Oh, great question. First I would say, there's been this big push to see Black lives mattering. Well, if Black lives matter in adulthood, Black lives should matter in childhood. It's not that schools are good because of the type of student or the type of family that attends. It's the type of resources that we put into those schools. I'll give you an example. There's a school here called Lockland. It's in East Nashville. At one point it was in the bottom 10 percent in the state. It had students that were middle to low income, and I mean you're talking 90 percent free or reduced lunch. So in the bottom 10 percent. Now it is in the top

5 percent of the state in performance. All it took was like six to eight families that decided "this is going to be our neighborhood school. Not only are we going to put our students here, but we're going to be a human resource for them." Started a PTO. They started fundraising. Got better support from the principal. They ask questions of teachers. They elevated the entire school in a number of ways simply because they were engaged. What I've seen happening, particularly with predominantly Black schools or in predominantly Black neighborhoods, is everyone that could opt out opted out. I grew up in North Nashville. Should have been zoned to Whites Creek. I think about the three other people on my street or close to my street that all went with me to MLK instead of to Whites Creek. How much would we have impacted that class of 2003? If our parents had put their fundraising capability, their knowledge about the system, understanding the questions they should be asking, offering support to our teachers . . . They pushed us to be better. They gave us ACT prep programming over the weekends and the summers. If that kind of support would have been more consistent at Whites Creek, how different Whites Creek's class of 2003 would have been. We don't see ourselves in the community as part of these systems, but we are. Because when we opt out and we say, Yeah, I love Black people, but my little Black child can't be with those little Black children, are we not sending a message to our children that says white is right? We pull resources from the community that we live in that we claim to love. So I've been trying to spread the message to everyone to choose your zone school. You can make it just as good as any magnet, any charter, any other optional school. And you can certainly make it as good as any private school because the twelve thousand dollars a year [per student] that we get for MNPS schools does not compare to the thirty thousand dollars a year that USN spends or the thirty-five thousand dollars a year that Ensworth spends, not to mention some of the other private schools in our area that we think are doing well, but who are still putting out students graduating with lower and lower ACTs, only earning a 15 or 16. There's a lot of misunderstanding and miscommunication about what public schools do.

MOORE: There's a lot of movement here in Nashville, right? We see our neighborhoods transform, which can be looked at as good or bad, right? You know, you can be a different type of gentrifier. What would you say to encourage them? If you're going to move to Twenty-Eighth in a tall and skinny, or if you're going to move into East Nashville or these other parts that have been historically Black, and have public schools that you could send your child to, send them there. What would you tell those people who are moving in and may not be from here, may not understand the neglect, may not understand the harm that has been done systemically to our public schools?

BUGGS: What I realized the last couple of years beyond the school board is that it's all about messaging. We don't do a good job of messaging about public schools because we often don't have enough funding to get communications professionals, but we've got to shift the way we talk about schools. That's what I've been telling everyone around me. Stop talking negatively about a school, especially if you haven't been in there. If you have been in there, think about the root of the problem that you see. If you see children acting inappropriately or maybe not meeting the level of academic success that you think they should be meeting, think about why they didn't get there. Every parent wants what's best for their child. Every child wants to be the best in the room. There's not a single child that wakes up and says, "You know what? Ima be stupid today." We just haven't resourced them. I think about some of our majority community, team members, my white neighbors, especially gentrifiers, who sometimes just don't know, you need to change their hearts and minds. Sometimes it's just having a conversation with them to explain the history of Nashville, to explain how diversity and how schools have kind of shifted. I also want to remind people that if you're going to call yourself an ally, I need you to be a true ally, and it is going to be uncomfortable because African Americans are going to be uncomfortable every single day. Then your level of allyship needs to match our uncomfortability. You saying to me that you bought South because you love the neighborhood, but you don't want your daughter to be the only white child in a school full of Black children. Welcome to our world. Do you really think your baby is going to be harmed by seeing people who don't look like them? You really think that you with all the resources that you bring having purchased a home in cash, while community members who have lived there for centuries can't afford to buy that home? Do you really think that they're going to do harm to you or your family? It was good enough for you to live there. It should be good enough for you to educate your child there.

MOORE: What does, in your perspective, educational justice mean for Nashville?

BUGGS: If it has to be one word, it would be resourcing. I remember with the last director we had, I don't care what anyone says, the thing that started his dismissal or his downfall in this city was because he tried to shift equity measures and no one wanted to listen. No one wanted to support it. So if you're familiar with Title One funding, Title One is the federal dollars that come down to cities, to school systems, to better support students who are socially, economically disadvantaged, whose families make below a certain amount of money. Well, you had schools that at one point were Title One schools, but gentrification switched that. So Lockland that was once sitting at, like I said, 90 percent free or reduced lunch, became 12 percent, but they were still getting about a hundred thousand dollars' worth of that Title One funding, right? And not to pick on Lockland, but that's just one easy example. He was trying to pull that money back and offer it to schools that were neediest. So instead of having any school that was at 50 percent free or reduced lunch, instead of them all getting the same amount of money, he wanted to shift more funding to schools that were at 75 percent free or reduced lunch or higher. Interestingly enough, that would have been all the predominantly Black or Brown schools in Nashville. Every single one is at 75 percent free or reduced lunch. So as soon as we want to start shifting dollars, parents said, "Well, hold on. Why does equity mean that I have to lose something?" Well, that's the definition of equity. We don't want to say it in that way. That means that those who have historically had resources many times that they really didn't qualify for based on guidelines, those now need to be shifted to schools and people who historically had not had it, but needed it. And instead of us saying, "That's a good measure, that's a good thing for us to do," there was outrage. I went to different communities and said, "Hey, I know you have a privilege in a certain way. So you can keep your kids out of an under-resourced school like a Pearl Cohn or Whites Creek. Well, you have that privilege, but there are so many families who don't. Can you please pick up for this?" And there was just silence.

MOORE: And that's where allyship is tested. If you say you are an ally to Black and Brown folks, this is your opportunity.

BUGGS: But, you know, the other side of that, though, that we often don't talk about when we speak on equity, is that there is a level of privilege that is outside of your race. So even though I might be low income and even though I have a child and I'm a single person, I still have education. I have three degrees. There's a certain level of privilege that comes with that. And so I've got to swallow that privilege and make sure that I better use my privilege to support students in my community, and in my area. There are people who are minorities who don't use their privilege, or at least don't recognize their privilege, and don't recognize that whatever decision they make may very well be harmful to the child next to them or the family next to them.

Scan the QR code to watch
the interview with Christiane
Buggs on YouTube.

CHAPTER SEVEN

JUDGE SHEILA CALLOWAY

Judge Sheila Calloway, a native of Louisville, Kentucky, came to Nashville in 1987. She received her BA degree in communications in 1991 and her JD in 1994, both from Vanderbilt University.

After graduating, she worked at the Metro Public Defender's Office in both the adult system as well as the juvenile system. In January 2004, she was appointed by Judge Betty Adams Green to the position of juvenile court magistrate. She was elected juvenile court judge in August 2014. She serves as an adjunct professor at Vanderbilt University Law School, Belmont Law School, and American Baptist College.

As a reader you will learn more about Judge Calloway's background and her passion to address children who end up in trouble, suspended from school, or sent to the juvenile justice system, and too often fall into the reality of embarking on a path to prison.

Judge Calloway shines a light on the need for us to find better ways to address behavioral problems without involving incarceration, leading to better outcomes for the kids and society. Judge Calloway believes putting our youth in jail is not the answer, and that we need to take a more restorative justice approach.

MOORE: Originally from Louisville, Kentucky. How was growing up there?

CALLOWAY: You know, growing up in Kentucky was awesome. I had the privilege to grow up with my parents, who are still married and together today fifty-four years later. They will be celebrating fifty-five years of marriage this year.

MOORE: Wow, everybody can't say that.

CALLOWAY: My parents taught me a lot about loving others and a lot about helping other people. When I grew up there, I thought we were super dysfunctional because they made us do everything together. You know, like Friday nights when my friends were at the games and hanging out, we had to go out to dinner with my parents and I'd be like, "Why does everybody else get to go out and I don't?" Since I was little, I probably was the one in the family that pushed that. I want to go with my friends, and I want to do this thing.

I would not understand until I stepped into the job of a public defender how important family was, and how important it was to have structured time together. How important that was. And all every time I can remember, they were always helping people. So like if some cousin who probably wasn't really a cousin needed a place to stay for a couple of weeks, right, they were at our house.

MOORE: Caring, loving, giving.

CALLOWAY: Caring, loving, giving, and they will give you the shirt off their back, give you a place to stay. Those things they implanted in me early on and that helped make who I am today.

MOORE: So what impact or influence did they have on you leading up to the role that you are in now, as the juvenile court judge?

CALLOWAY: So other than just learning how to help people and to love people and to help people get a second chance, there wasn't much else about the law or the legal system that they influenced me on.

My mom was one of those people that kept everything me and my sister did. So every paper, every little project, she would just box them up. First grade box, second grade box. And one day I went to get my stuff and I was looking at my fourth grade box, and I wrote a paper in fourth grade that said, "When I grow up I want to be a lawyer and help people." And I have absolutely no idea what made me say that, there's no lawyers in our family at the time. The only thing I could possibly think is that we had some kind of career day at school and I heard a lawyer talk, and that's probably what I wanted to do.

I came to Nashville to go to school at Vanderbilt. I went both for my undergraduate degree, which was in communications, and then my law degree as well. I went to Vanderbilt seven years in a row.

MOORE: Nashville is It City, as some people like to call it. But in your position, I know you get to see a different perspective of Nashville on a daily basis that your normal everyday people don't get to see. Can you break down to your everyday role and the process of your job?

CALLOWAY: Absolutely. I have the best job in Nashville, absolutely the best as a juvenile court judge. I have the best opportunity to influence so many families and children in our community, more so than anybody else. And that's why I absolutely love my job.

I have 125 staff employees, give or take a few. We run a detention facility that I'm responsible for that has about eighty employees. They house on average about thirty youth. A 24/7 facility, and we have the opportunity and ability to partner with so many different agencies around our community to make sure that all of our families and their children are doing well.

I actually do hear cases. I sit on the bench every day. I usually hear cases from nine o'clock in the morning, till four or five in the evening. With a lunch break. I gotta have a lunch break. I always tell the litigants there in the courtroom, "You want me to take a break for lunch. Because if you don't, it's not happy, it's not pretty on the other side of no lunch." So I do hear cases every day.

The nature of the cases that we hear, it's basically three categories. The first category is a third of the cases dealing with parents who are not married. So if you are not married, never been married, you have kids together, any issues that you have with your children and co-parenting, they are heard in juvenile court.

MOORE: I want to break this down, because this is real deep. My dad is great. My dad is still great to this day. I think especially for a lot of Black men, there is a struggle when Black fathers want to be in their kid's life. That sometimes it's not them not wanting to be there, but it could be actually the mother preventing them, creating barriers. And I know that's not always the case, but this is popular talk, especially among Black men. You hear horror stories like baby mama drama or just mama drama and things like that, especially when it comes to the custody of the kids. Can you break it down for us? That process on joint custody and child support and things like that?

CALLOWAY: Absolutely. And I love to talk about this, because I definitely know that perception and that perception was real. There were a lot of men who were stepping forward to be fathers and to be the best father that they can, to spend time with their children. And sometimes it's the mother, sometimes it's just a system in general that prevents that from happening. What I know, based on the statistics and the studies across the nation, is that children who grow up with parents who are active in their lives have the least likelihood of entering into the criminal justice system. To prevent problems from happening, and prevent crimes, and prevent our young people from having contact with the system, I need to work on the parent. I need to make sure that that child has both parents in their life.

The law still says that if you are unmarried, the mother is presumed to be the guardian. The law still says that. However, once the father steps up to say, "I am the father, I want to be part of it," then we have to start with a basic understanding that both parents should have the maximum participation in their child's life as possible. So both parents should have maximum participation. For me, that means you all start off evenly. And then things make a difference. Like, if there's a big difference if the child has to get to school and, you know, the father's in another county, we may not be able to do week on week off. Or if, you know, there's other questionable things that happened, may not be able to do it. But what the law says now is that you all start with each person having the maximum participation. And so it really depends on who the judge is, how they interpret maximum participation.

But me and the magistrates that work for me all recognize that means equal time, because you know sometimes mothers on the case that come into the courtroom they say, "Well he should only get to see him every other weekend." Let's talk about that, what does that mean? So if you are dating someone, and you really want to get to know this person, and you really like them, and you're thinking maybe we can do a little more, and you tell the person that you're dating that you really want to spend time with them, but you can only spend time with them every other weekend, how's that make you feel? Not appreciated. If I'm only seeing every other weekend, the time I get to see you, I'm relearning everything that I learned two weeks ago, and it takes time.

MOORE: So what is that process?

CALLOWAY: We are making the process so much easier than what it used to be. We have labeled this year [2021] the "Year for the Parent." We are trying to do more to make people understand that it is okay to step up and try to be a parent. You don't even necessarily have to have a lawyer to do this. You can go to the juvenile court website, and the form's on there that you would have to fill out. If you don't think you have enough to pay for the filing of a petition, you can ask to be declared indigent and we can waive some of the costs for the filing. We do have to charge for serving the other parent, but other than that we can waive a lot of the cost. So it doesn't cost that much.

And we recommend that you come down early, often as early as possible. Because court hearings do take a while. The sooner you get down there, the better. The parental-assistant court specialists are all trained as mediators. So you can file your petition, you can say, "I would love to try mediation," the parent gets served. They say, "I'll agree to mediation." You can do mediation before your case even goes to court, work out an agreement as to what type of parenting time each parent gets, and just have it announced when you come back to court. So things can happen a lot quicker if both parties are in agreement. If they're not in agreement, then there are going to be court hearings. That may take some time, but from the very first time you go to court, there will be an interim order as to the parenting time. So that usually sets it from the beginning as the maximum time possible, unless you give a good reason why you shouldn't until the next court order.

Another third of the cases that we have are the cases where parents are alleged to have abused or neglected their children. That's about a third of the cases. So literally, what I tell people is, when I think about what I do in juvenile court, two-thirds of the stuff I do is about what the parents are doing to their children.

MOORE: What are some of the craziest cases that you've heard?

CALLOWAY: These are difficult cases. These are the ones that emotionally make you hurt. You know, we had a parent who had a, unfortunately, a drug addiction that was hard to overcome. And this is probably one of the worst cases I've had of child abuse where the parent, in order to, I guess, feed their addiction, was allowing their child to be used.

That's a difficult case, because our job, we don't prosecute the parents for anything that happens in criminal court. But what our job is to do, is to figure out what's best for that child, or if that child should remain with that parent and get some services in, or whether that child should go to a relative or to a family friend or someone in the community, or whether that child has to go into the custody of the state, the foster care system. And you know, to be truthful, our state isn't designed to take care of children. That's the worst option. You would love to be able to have children go back to their families, but sometimes the offenses are so extreme or the drug addiction is so deep that it's hard to get them to a point where they can actually parent their child. And those are hard cases, super hard cases.

MOORE: These are things that actually go on in our own communities.

CALLOWAY: A lot of our parents are driven to do things because they've been left out. If they are homeless, if they are unable to get good meals, food, you know, we have so many people in our community that live in food deserts, and if you can't feed your child, what happens to that child? That child ends up becoming neglected. And a lot of times, it's not because they want to neglect. They were unable to get themselves in a position in our community where they can really be a good parent.

MOORE: I want to talk to you about a school to prison pipeline, and how your court impacts that and in what way.

CALLOWAY: There is definitely no question about it that there is a school to prison pipeline. What we know is that youth who are expelled or suspended from school have a higher likelihood of ending up in the criminal justice system, and it makes common sense. Because if I'm suspended from school and I'm going home, probably my parent or parents have to work and they're not home to supervise.

MOORE: How can we keep kids out of jail?

CALLOWAY: There are so many things that we can do as a community to keep our youth out of jails. And I will. I am happy to say that I started this job in 2014. We've been very intentional about keeping our records and seeing how many youth we have getting charged with things. We looked at 2013, how many youth were being arrested in our community? The numbers were around four thousand. At the end of 2020, that number was down to one thousand. So we literally have decreased the number of youth who are being arrested by 60-something percent. And it's not just a testament to me, but it's a testament to us collaborating with the schools, with the police, with our community-based organizations. Just with the whole community, about how arresting youth is not the answer. It doesn't serve a purpose, and the more that you put a youth in the system, the longer they stay in and usually the worse they get.

Locking people up doesn't solve problems. It doesn't get to the heart of why that child did that offense. So let's figure out why they did the offense, and then we can determine what we need to do about it.

MOORE: Last question. You have a lot of power. You are a decision maker in the city of Nashville. How do you make sure that you're using your power in the best way possible, that benefits the community, that benefits parents, and benefits kids?

CALLOWAY: So, you know, I believe that those who are in power have to use it to the good of the whole community. For me, it's my spiritual base, and for me, it's knowing that each and every day I'm doing things that God would be pleased with. So that keeps me grounded. I am in this position because this is the time or season that God put me here. It's nothing I did on my own, nothing that just happened, but God intentionally had me in this position for a reason. I know each and every day, I'm here to make decisions that affect positively this community. That's why I strongly believe that every day, as long as I keep God first, that I'll be able to use the power that God has given me for the benefit of everybody.

Scan the QR code to watch
the interview with Judge
Sheila Calloway on YouTube.

CHAPTER EIGHT

DAWN DEANER

Dawn Deaner is the founder and executive director of the Choosing Justice Initiative. Before launching CJI in November 2018, Dawn spent ten years as the metropolitan public defender for Nashville-Davidson County, Tennessee, and eleven years before that as an assistant public defender in Nashville.

As Nashville's chief public defender, Dawn was a tireless advocate for her clients and their right to high-quality, effective legal representation. Beginning early in her tenure, she fostered a culture of client-centered representation and encouraged staff to treat every client like they would want their own family treated.

Dawn acknowledges the reality that public defenders have contributed to mass incarceration by not doing enough to insist that people without wealth have access to meaningful legal representation. Dawn questions her own effectiveness as an elected official and how the system may play a role in how effective she or anyone could really be to build a better and safer community.

Can one person change a system? How many people does it take to make systemic change in the criminal legal system?

MOORE: What happens in the public defender's office?

DEANER: What happens? Lots happens in the public defender's office. You know, I often think about it as the emergency room of the criminal legal system, frankly. It never stops. People never stop getting arrested, and the vast majority of people who get arrested can't afford to hire lawyers, and so there's just a constant turn of new people being arrested, coming into jails, coming into the office. And the public defender's office's job is to try to help those individuals get justice. Maybe I think that my attitude about getting justice has changed over twenty-five years.

MOORE: What is justice to you?

DEANER: I think it's a really good question that nobody ever really asks. We hear the phrase *criminal justice system*, which is not a phrase I use anymore. I refer to the court as the *criminal legal system*. I have a colleague who refers to it as the *criminal punishment system*, and I think that that's probably the most descriptive phrase for it.

It's not unusual these days to hear people referring to it as the criminal legal or criminal punishment system. Because that is really the only kind of justice that happens within the court system for the most part, is punishment, which is one concept of justice. But, you know, I went to law school, and I don't recall ever having a conversation during three years in law school about what justice is. I think it is not a question that many people think about, and certainly not many lawyers. For me, justice has come to mean something much more philosophical, and is about how people live in community with each other, in relationship with each other, in a voluntary way. And I think *voluntary* is important, particularly in the context of US culture. How we live together, in relationship with each other; the agreements that we make about how we will do that peacefully; and most importantly, how we will deal with violations of that agreement. Because it's one thing to agree that I'm going to let you be in peace, and you're going to let me be in peace, but what happens when that peace gets disturbed? What happens when you do something that harms me, violates the agreement that we had? How do we deal with that violation? To me, that's what justice is really about, and I think what our court system has long been about is power and control and punishment and oppression. And so it is no surprise, then, that the kind of justice that happens in the court system for people who are perceived as violating the code of conduct is purely punishment.

MOORE: How did you use the power that you had in the public defender's office to best serve Nashville?

DEANER: During the time that I was there, I always had power. Lawyers have power, specifically related to their knowledge of the court system, right? So when I was a line attorney, I tried my best to use my power as a lawyer to serve, and help, and get good outcomes for my clients. Once I became the head of the office, that obviously changes. You develop, in some respects, a greater sense of power to make systemic changes. So instead of helping one client or serving one client, or trying to get one client justice, you have a platform to do that writ large, run for a much broader population of people. And so I tried to do that as the public defender, and in all honesty, it took me probably two to three years to even understand the power that I had in the platform that I had, and to come to learn the difference between managing and leading. My responsibility as the leader of the public defender's office was to speak truth, first and foremost, which is not something that happens in the court system nearly as often as it should . . . certainly I don't think it happens. I had always struggled with the idea that our clients called us "public pretenders."

MOORE: Yeah, public defenders get a bad rep.

DEANER: It's complicated. Public defenders have the reputation, the stereotype, that exists for a reason. As a public defender, I felt I had to own that and deal with that, and acknowledge it and interrogate it. Why do we have that reputation? And the truth is the public defense system in this country was never set up to succeed at providing equal justice to people who don't have money to hire lawyers. I think that's a systemic issue. But I think also, it was never set up to exist in community, in solidarity with the people who we represent. There is this power dynamic that exists, and as long as the system works for public defenders, then we have something to lose if we do speak up. So I felt like the most important thing I could do as public defender, and using my power, is to invite that conversation with the individuals who we were representing and still represent. To say, "What do we need to be doing better? What are we doing wrong? How are we not helping you speak? How are we not speaking for you the way we need to speak for you? How are we not fighting for you?"

For me, ultimately the most important issue became reducing our workloads, because I knew that, as long as we have too many clients, we can't provide each client with the kind of zealous defense that they need and deserve. We would never be anything but public pretenders, and we would never have the trust and faith of the people there, of our clients, of their families, or the larger communities from where they live. So fundamentally, I felt like we needed to change that, so we cut caseloads and started turning clients away, which was a very difficult thing. We can talk about this later, but when the public defender doesn't represent you, there's an entirely different system of indigent defense. Well, that is in many respects worse than the public defender option. So we knew that when we turned clients away, they were going to be funneled into a system that also was not working well and harmed people. We started a client Advisory Board to try to get input from individuals who may not necessarily have been represented by our office, but who had lived the experience of going through the court system with a court-appointed lawyer and had things to say about what the problems were, and advice to offer about how we could be doing better for our clients.

The third thing I would say is that I learned that as long as you sit in rooms and say no to everything, at tables where people in other positions of power are . . . as long as you sit in those rooms and don't say anything, or just say no to everything, you're not going to get very far. So I learned a lot from watching other elected officials at those tables. They had ideas, they brought ideas, and they said, "This is what I see needs to be done to address some of the systemic issues that are happening."

MOORE: So what are some things that Nashville should be talking about when it comes to the criminal justice system that we're not talking about? What are some topics that we are just avoiding here in

Nashville, when it comes to our criminal justice system, or criminal legal system?

DEANER: So, to me, the most important question that we should all be asking is: How is this helping anybody? How is it making anybody healthier? How is it keeping us safer? How is it delivering accountability? Ultimately, is this representative of justice? Those are really specific questions that I think anybody looking at our court system needs to be asking, because we spend a lot of money on our court system, and the court system is tied in with policing. It's tied in with jails. It's tied in with probation. The Nashville People's Budget Coalition really has been central in, I think, trying to start educating Nashvillians about it. And the Black Nashville Assembly is a new organization that's really working on issues around primarily defunding police, but their perspective is much broader in terms of defunding law enforcement in the whole system.

MOORE: Let's talk about the money because I'm just fascinated by the number of fees, court costs, attorney fees, probationary fees. Once you get arrested and go to jail, people stay in jail for the simple fact that they can't afford to get out. And me and you could have the same crime, same criminal background, and have drastically different bail amounts. How does that happen? What is going on?

DEANER: If you look at it historically, it does make sense. Bails generally are designed to benefit the wealthy and to oppress those who are not wealthy.

If you want to go backward: Jim Crow. Go back to convict leasing. Go back to slavery. The idea of convict leasing is the thing that comes to my mind, most prevalently, when I think about costs associated with the court system. Costs, fines, fees; and if you can't pay them, it used to be under convict leasing. Well, then you would be leased out to the landowner to go work off your debt. I set your bail at $50 on a loitering charge, which is really what came to rise. The time of convict leasing in this country was reconstruction, post-reconstruction, and in the South in particular, this concept of *vagrancy*, which was largely African Americans who are looking for work. Standing on the street corner. The same thing still happens today. We're standing on a street corner, you have interaction with police, but if I arrest you for vagrancy or public loitering, and I set your bail at $50 and you can't afford to pay that bail, then you are much more likely to go to court and plead guilty to that. What we see today, in the current system, are just the carryovers and the legacy of all these same practices in a different form. Which is demoralizing, but I think also, if we understand its roots, it helps us to understand why we need to change it.

MOORE: So, I want to go backward a little bit. You were the public defender for Davidson County, Nashville, ten-year run. Then you said, "I'm done." Why be done with that role?

DEANER: I've been asked that question a lot. I'm gonna blame Judge Calloway, who I know was on *Deep Dish*. What happened was she invited me to go to California with her, to learn about restorative justice. That was such a powerful experience for me, to learn about a different kind of justice than what I was seeing in the courtroom, and what I had been participating in for the last eighteen years of my life. I had this moment and I started thinking, "How much good have I really done for anybody in my career? How have I really helped anybody? Have I made anybody better?" Those are the questions that I think people need to be asking themselves about justice. That really started me thinking about what I want to do for the rest of my career. Do I want to try something different? So that was kind of the impetus that got me thinking about, maybe I really don't need to be the public defender for the rest of my career. I think on top of that, working in government can be really restrictive, and there are rules of that bureaucracy that you have to follow. One of them that particularly struck me was our inability at the public defender's office to be able to serve people in dealing with their problems.

Beyond whatever their criminal case was, the reality is that people who have been arrested and are involved in the criminal legal system often have overlapping issues. And if we really wanted to be about helping people problem solve and get past what's brought them into the criminal legal system, oftentimes they need help to navigate other legal arenas and our hands were tied. We just couldn't do that. That model to me just doesn't make any sense. I didn't have a whole lot of faith I could, within the public defender model, expand what we were doing. And I wasn't really sure, like I said, that I wanted to seed it in a government office. That was the journey I was on, really educating myself about things none of us were taught in high school or college related to the government role in oppressions, and learning much more about the history of this country. That's why I was a public defender, is that I cared about the people who we were representing and who were impacted by the system. None of them really have any respect for public defenders . . . frankly, there's not a whole lot of respect for government. I just got more and more uncomfortable being connected and affiliated and associated with government. The government and all its associated systems are set up in the way they are set up for reasons that are about oppression and racism and capitalism, and for reasons that perpetuate harm on communities and people who are oppressed. I wasn't sure I wanted to be part of that anymore.

Scan the QR code to watch
the interview with Dawn
Deaner on YouTube.

PART IV

WHITE PEOPLE

CHAPTER NINE

TIM WISE

Many of you may ask, What role can I play in social justice as a white person? Some may wonder if white people should play a role at all.

Tim Wise is among the most prominent anti-racist writers and educators in the United States. He has spent the past twenty-five years speaking to audiences in all fifty states, on over 1,500 college and high school campuses, at hundreds of professional and academic conferences, and to community groups across the country. He has trained corporate, government, entertainment, media, law enforcement, military, and medical industry professionals on methods for dismantling racial inequity in their institutions and has provided anti-racism training to educators and administrators nationwide and internationally. He appears regularly on CNN and MSNBC to discuss racial politics and is the host of the podcast *Speak Out with Tim Wise*.

Wise gives us a detailed journey of his path into anti-racist work and how his whiteness played a role throughout that journey. He showcases the privilege that he even has in being able to address social justice issues as a white man while knowing that his job is to address white people.

MOORE: So one of the first questions I have for you, Tim, is what role did faith, family, friends, your community play into your journey around what you are doing now, especially around being an anti-racism activist?

WISE: I guess all of that had some role to play. Family, a huge role. I've talked about this a lot. I grew up in Nashville, and I was born in 1968. I went to preschool at Tennessee State in the early childhood ed program at TSU, and the reason that I did that . . . I didn't live in North Nashville, I didn't live around TSU. I lived in Green Hills, but my mom made the very deliberate decision to send me to TSU for preschool. This would have been around 1972. So at three, almost four, to start a preschool program there, and she did that, you know, very deliberately wanted me to have a more integrated environment. Wanted me to not always be the norm in the room, you know. I was going to be starting public school a couple years after that, and she knew that those public schools had just really become integrated. You know, Nashville Public Schools didn't really fully integrate until 1971, seventeen years after *Brown v. Board*. So by 1974, when I was gonna be starting first grade, she wanted me to have a context for integrated education.

And so at TSU, I was one of only three not-Black kids in the class, and the women that ran the program were Black women, which also, you know, made a difference in terms of just socializing me to respect Black authority. So I think those decisions were really instrumental because it meant that when I saw Black kids who were my friends now being treated differently, it was not just people that I'd read about, or abstractions. These were people that I had some relationship with, seeing them mistreated in the schools, that affected me in a way that it probably wouldn't have if I hadn't known them. And years later, when I'm working as a community organizer in public housing, Black women are the voices in community I've learned to respect . . . Black women, going back to when I was a little kid, so that was a big piece.

The faith piece is interesting. You know, I was raised Jewish. I went to Temple till I was about thirteen, and then I dropped out of Hebrew school. So I'm a Hebrew school dropout, which my rabbi, I'm sure he's very proud of. I wouldn't say that faith per se had a huge role, but I think being Jewish certainly. In this town, you know, at every four-way stop it's three churches and a Walgreens. You definitely grow up with a sense of otherness if you're in the South and you're Jewish, and I think at the time that I was growing up here there were probably about five thousand Jews in Nashville max, and it may not even be that much more now, I don't know, but certainly had a sense of otherness. I mean, I remember being treated very differently in public schools by teachers who thought it was appropriate to try to make us pray in their tradition. First of all, it's not appropriate to make us pray at all. The Supreme Court had already said that in 1962, but they tried. So I remember always feeling a bit like an outsider, but luckily, and this is really critical, I'd had that TSU experience and I could see the way my Black friends were treated as outsiders, so I didn't get so wrapped up in my otherness that I couldn't see other people's otherness. I could actually empathize in a way because I was having this outsider experience, and that gave me a little bit of insight into the fact that my Black friends were being tracked into the low-level track. They were being disciplined more harshly. So I was catching hell, but they were too, and I was able to see that.

MOORE: You were a community organizer. How was that for you?

WISE: It was critical to my development in the work that I do. Ultimately, I only did it for about fifteen to eighteen months, but it was an incredible learning experience because I had to learn and it's particularly humbling for white men that become organizers, because the thing about organizing is, you know, having been trained to do it and having done it right, it's really not about you. It's really not about your voice. You're trying to help other people find their voice, and you're trying to get them to discover the power and the capabilities that they have to exercise autonomy in their community, and self-determination. But when you're a white man in this country, you're really encouraged to think that it is about your voice. So you go in and you fix it, or you go in and you offer the solution, or you go in and you tell them what you think. And as an organizer, you have to have a very, very different mentality.

First, I worked with an organization that was a family and children's advocacy group, that was rooted in anti-racism training from the People's Institute for Survival and Beyond in New Orleans. Everybody that went through this had to have an explicit anti-racism background, which is different, because not all organizing models emphasize racism. Lots of them emphasize economic injustice, of course, but sometimes race is on the periphery. Ours was very explicit, which was incredibly important for me. Secondly, the adage within organizing is you don't go until you're asked in, and when you're asked in you go. And so for me, I had to be shepherded through. I was working in public housing communities in New Orleans and it would have made absolutely zero sense for me to just roll up in this community and say, "I'm here to help." Literally the only white folks that looked like me that they saw were either cops or social workers. So they're not going to trust me. Only way that I could gain the trust of the community and interact with the community in a productive way was someone who was a resident in the community, who worked with our organization, brought me in, introduced me to people, vouched for me. Then I had to demonstrate that I was trustworthy over the course of time, and it took a minute, so I had to subordinate my ego a lot, and it was a really good experience. I learned the importance of seeing wisdom in these spaces where I knew it existed. It's like, you didn't have to tell me there was wisdom in those communities, but when you're actually hearing it, when you're actually hearing folks that have a high school diploma or less in many cases explaining the class system, explaining race better than the college course that you took two years ago or five years ago, then you start to realize how much we're missing as a society by not tapping into that wisdom.

MOORE: One of the most exciting things I am interested in learning about you is why? A white man growing up in Nashville, Tennessee, political science major, probably could have been anything else that you wanted to be and make butt loads of money, doing whatever you wanted to do. Why anti-racism activist, why this work?

WISE: Well, you know, part of it is that background of having those early relationships and that early awareness that was the result of my mom making that decision to send me to TSU. It was also, I think, early on as I was coming up and I had these close connections, I saw certain things that just stick with you.

For me it was when I was ten or eleven, and I was playing baseball. I played ball here in Nashville. It's funny, you know, I went to Hebrew school with all the other Jewish kids and they were all playing at the JCC, and I was playing ball at the Y. So I was playing basketball at the Y and I was real good until you had to be tall. So after about sixth grade, I was done. But I was really good at baseball. And so the same guys that I played basketball with in the same league, same coach, we had a baseball team and so I would say that team was about thirteen guys and probably nine were Black kids and four were white. And we went out to play a scrimmage one weekend out of town, like, out in Joelton, which isn't really that far, but twenty-five minutes or something.

Its Joelton 1980. So it's a semi-rural part of the Nashville area and we roll in not really thinking anything of it. We go out there, we are going to scrimmage against this team. We showed up, we only had like, eight guys show up because somebody got sick. So we didn't have enough to fill a whole team, but we were like, look, we still want to play, just a scrimmage. We'll collapse left field and right field, just two left and right center, and we'll play, and y'all can play nine if you want. We don't care, we just want the practice. Then they were like, "We're not going to do it," and they didn't want to play. But that wasn't really what the deal was. It wasn't really that. We learn that very quickly because as we were leaving these guys, not all of them, but several of the players on the other team surrounded our car. We had a coach that would just like jam all of us in his car and, you know, no seat belt, no safety, nothing. We just had that like nine guys, eight guys, and they surrounded the car, they're yelling at us. They're calling the Black kids the n-word, they're calling the white kids n-word lovers, and all that. And I'm eleven or whatever and I'm seeing this.

For me, that was the first time that I had really seen that level of overt racism against my friends and teammates. This wasn't some abstract thing I read. This was happening right in front of me. And having white people tell me, You as a white person have crossed this line and now you're on that side of the line and we're going to make you pay for it. To me, that stuff . . . I mean there's a reason you remember those things, because how many things happen to you when you're eleven and you don't remember them? But that stuck with me. So that didn't necessarily make me want to do this as a career. That's a longer discussion. But for me, that was always going to be in the back of my mind, that I had some obligations because of those early experiences.

And then when I graduated from college I was in Louisiana. David Duke, former Klan leader, white supremacist neo-Nazi was running for US Senate and governor, and I was involved in the campaigns against him. Even though he lost, he got six out of ten white people to vote for him. So that's one of those moments where you realize. Just like those boys in Joelton, rather than hate them—which would have been very easy and I did for a while—but rather I came to really see them. Where did they learn that? They learned that at home. So they were the victims of the collateral damage of the conditioning of their parents, and their parents were the collateral damage, the conditioning of their parents. So, I came to have this . . . not sympathy, but compassion for the fact that white folks are being damaged by our own mindset of white supremacy. And then, when you see 675,000 white people in Louisiana vote for a guy they know is a Nazi . . . now you really understand. Like, that's pretty heavy, because I know they're not all Nazis. But they're voting for a dude they know is. They're like, "Yeah I know he's a Nazi, but gosh, you know, I really do like what he has to say about welfare recipients." Wow, really? Because he's a Nazi. You heard that right there like, "Yeah, I know, but I really liked what he said about affirmative action." Like, yeah, but he's a Nazi. You understand that, right?

So that's that moment where you go, Okay, I have some work to do. Not to save Black folks in Louisiana. Black folks in Louisiana were clear, "We're going to stop him. Y'all clearly are not. We will, so you're welcome. We're going to save y'all from yourself." The question was not who's going to save those Black kids that were in the car with me. They were going to save themselves. If they had to get out with baseball bats and defend themselves, they would have done it. The question was, who's going to save those white children whose parents taught them that hatred. That's my job. That's certainly not your job. You can't liberate white people, you got to just stay alive and keep moving yourself. The only people that can liberate white people from this nonsense that we've done to others and to ourselves are other white people.

MOORE: What have you learned about yourself during this journey? What are some of the things that you have figured out about yourself that you didn't know?

WISE: It has demonstrated to me that I don't have a great work ethic. People think that's weird because I write a lot of articles, and I've written eight books, and I give all these talks. But the truth is, I'm really not a very hard worker. And I'm not trying to say that like as a matter of false modesty. What's that about? Well, that's a lot about white privilege and male privilege. And I'm not saying that I'm not good at the things that I do, but I just feel like sometimes I find myself not as focused as I wish I were.

MOORE: I know you mentioned earlier about the impact that your mom had, you know, on the work that you're doing now, and putting you in the situation so you can better see and understand things that, especially being a white man in America, that you probably wouldn't have been able to recognize and see if you had not made those decisions. What role did your father play?

WISE: Again I want to give credit and look at the good and the bad of all this. It's a complicated relationship I had with both my parents, actually. Look, I make my living running my mouth. I make my living performing in a way. When I get up and speak, that's a performance. Well, my ability to do that and do that effectively I'm sure owes a lot to the fact that my dad was a stand-up comic and an actor for most of his professional life. My oral communication skills come from that. So, if it weren't for him, I wouldn't be doing what I'm doing, I'm sure, at least not in the way that I'm doing it.

On the other hand, there was a lot of dysfunction there. My dad was an alcoholic and addict. He's been in recovery now for many, many years, but growing up certainly was not. So I dealt with a lot of that chaos and a lot of that isolation that comes with that chaos. I was an only child, so it was just me dealing with that dysfunction. And like I said, I think that is the kind of thing that, when you have your own family and you're trying to figure out how to be a better man, or a better husband, or a better father, just a better human being, you will sometimes fall back into the only modeling that you ever saw. Even when you know that's not effective, good modeling. So there's a lot of that I struggle with all the time. And again, some of those struggles I win, some of those struggles I've lost, but they're ongoing, they're constant, and that's not just me, that's for anyone. So, I think that my father's implicated for good and for bad, and who I've become now politically, ideologically, philosophically, my mom and dad were on the same page around these things.

So my mom made that sort of active decision to send me to Tennessee State, but my mom and dad were on the same page politically as I was growing up about issues. My mom and dad were both a little bit too young to have been activists in the civil rights era, but my dad was very progressive, came from a progressive family. My mom actually came from a very conservative family, so she was the one that was more rebelling against her folks. My dad is the Jewish side of the family, and they were much more liberal, much more progressive. That's not to say, though, that they had all their stuff together. I've talked about that as well, in a lot of my work, that there were still a lot of blind spots that the family had. So I would say that, in both some really good ways and in some problematic ways, both my parents are implicated in who I became.

Scan the QR code to watch
the interview with Tim Wise
on YouTube.

CHAPTER TEN

WILL ACUFF

On the surface, Will Acuff would be the poster child for what a white savior looks like. But as we take a deeper dive, we learn more about Will's journey and commitment to community through the love of neighbor, which takes the form of educational and economic equity, creating a city where all can thrive.

Will was born in Durham, North Carolina, but grew up in Hudson, Massachusetts. He graduated from North Carolina State University and has his master's degree from Reformed Theological Seminary.

Will is passionate about the Grace of God through Christ, and how that grace invites us to live a life of sacrificial love toward our city and our neighbors.

MOORE: If you look at Will on the surface, white man has a faith-based nonprofit in Nashville that primarily helps people of color, Black people in low socio-economic areas. Father that has an adopted Black child with special needs, disability, and Christian, faith-based—and he helps people. So, on a surface that spells like White Savior all the way. That's top-notch white saviorism.

ACUFF: Like an after-school special movie. This is like a Hallmark special.

MOORE: From a 1 to 10, the only reason it would be a 9.5 of white saviorism is because you adopted domestically. If it wasn't for that, it would have been a 12 out of 10.

ACUFF: He's checking all the boxes. This guy thinks he's the Great White Hope.

MOORE: On the surface, when I see it, it's like there has to be something more. And after doing my research it's definitely something more, so let's get into that. Let's talk about white saviorism. How do you avoid that? How do you make sure you don't just check off those boxes?

ACUFF: I mean, I've got a lot of answers to this question. Depends on where you want to go, right? I'll start from a kind of a really nerdy answer, which is what I would describe as having an asset-based community model instead of a needs-based. Because the needs-based says, Look at this neighborhood. We see XYZ problems and we assume we know how to fix it. We're going to bring in a middle-class efficiency framework to fix those problems, and often that also means we're going to bring in white supremacy. We're going to bring in standards that are developed for the white community. That and paternalism can sometimes be in, with, and under that vibe.

On the asset-based model, you start from a different approach and you say: What is already happening that's incredible? How do we amplify the good? And so shifting that mindset doesn't guarantee you're going to get away from the white saviorism, but it does mean you're starting from a much better position. That would be my first answer. An example of this is literacy rates in Nashville. Two-thirds of our kids aren't reading at grade level. That hasn't moved significantly in over twenty years and that primarily affects low-income communities, which in Nashville means Black and Brown kids. You could start with the problem, or you could say, Hey, our kids are amazing and creative and are making content on every social platform you can think of, and grown-ups are sitting at home going, This is amazing, I don't understand how any of this works. So, we can start from the asset-based. "Oh my gosh, incredible creators. How can we get at the literacy challenges through this amazing asset of youth creativity?" Those kind of things then put the kid front and center, versus the kid is the problem or the kid is the victim. So that's what I mean by the asset base.

My personal answer to the white savior thing—and you brought it up as soon as I get in the back, you were talking about my trip to Nairobi—the real story for me is I came to Faith at age six, raised as a pastor's kid, and raised outside of Boston where my whole family had moved to start a church. It started in the office of a gas station. We're not talking fancy. We're talking like bring your own chair, maybe your tambourine.

MOORE: Bring everything that you need to worship.

ACUFF: Yes, because we don't have anything here. But I saw that grow like crazy from like '85 to '95. And I saw gospel as lived-out adventure toward love of God and love of neighbor. And when I came to college in the South—I went to NC State—that was the first time I was really in the mix with like Southern church culture and it was kind of a shock to my system.

I had grown up with some solid doctrinal truth, but I would say I had no theology of love of neighbor. I would describe what I had been taught as, again, some really solid stuff, but love of neighbor was essentially share the gospel or occasionally go on a mission trip for like five days that makes you feel great. That is fully white saviorism. Where there's no relationship, where it makes you feel better, it probably victimizes somebody.

I had that mindset until I got a chance to go on this trip to Nairobi, led by an epidemiologist from UNC who was an expert in the spread of the HIV/AIDS pandemic and all the factors that influence that. For six months prior to going on that trip, we met at his house. He, his wife—and she was a general practitioner—we met at their house and we read doctrinal papers. We read economic papers. We read things about how North American policy influences sub-Saharan African poverty, stuff that I had never heard about, just oblivious. Then we went to Nairobi and we all divide it up. So it wasn't like we're going to stay in this nice hotel. I was staying with a Kenyan family on the edge of this slum with no running water. I had never been out of the US before. I was immersed and my worldview dissolved. *Blew up* is a better phrase.

I remember coming back from that trip and almost having a visceral . . . like, vomiting when I walked into my parents' middle-class home. It had never seemed too opulent before, and now it seemed opulent. And I was like, if this Jesus is real, if that's who I say I follow, this cannot also exist in the world. This much brokenness, this much disparity. And it was one of those moments where, it's cliché, the white kid has to go to Africa to realize poverty's real. That's a trope, but it led to not a "I am going to fix it." It led to, "I'm going to learn."

Something that I'm really passionate about is the idea of cultural humility. When you move toward the neighbors with cultural humility you come with a heart of learning in a posture of, "I don't know, show me." It might take some time to develop trust and long-term relationships. But you get away from that hero mentality and you get into what we describe at Corners to Corners as a neighbor-first approach. This is what I'm super passionate about is the white Christian, especially the Evangelical world, has historically had this "we have the answers, we can fix you and we can fix you quickly," but also move at the speed of efficiency, not the speed of relationship. And the way nonprofits have been structured both in terms of leadership methodology, but also most critically in terms of fundraising, is this tragically broken model. I think we can destroy and rebuild.

So in the course of all this learning, I got my master's in biblical theology so I could understand and talk better about this stuff. And one of the things they talk about is the anthropology of man. Like who is mankind, per the way the Bible describes it. Genesis to Revelation, what do we see? And what the Bible describes is, we're created in the image of God. So, on some level, more beautiful than we can fathom. One theologian put it like this: "You've never met a mere mortal." So you can imagine, we should be freaking out about each other. When I see a new human, I should be like, "You're incredible!"

We should be on some level having that experience of each other. But simultaneously the Bible talks about how we're broken. We hurt ourselves. We hurt those who we're close to. We hurt our community. But we're both of those things. We're not one or the other, we're both.

And in the nonprofit fundraising world . . . Have you ever been to one of those fundraising banquets?

MOORE: Yeah.

ACUFF: So the way those fundraising banquets work in the Christian world is we rip this image of man apart. One person, that donor, gets to come in bearing the image of God and image of wealth in the world. And one person gets to come in bearing the image of victimhood, the image of brokenness, and it creates distance and pity. And it says, "Hey, donor, you get to be the hero." It's nothing different than the typical Cadillac commercial.

MOORE: Exactly.

ACUFF: Like you see the Cadillac commercials, it's like rakish young man loosens tie. It's a beautiful city street. Hops into his Cadillac and in seconds he's on a mountain road. Where does dude live? How close is the city to the mountains? But then he's driving, and you're watching like, I'm kind of like that dude, right? I'm master of my domain. And then he pulls into this modern home, and a supermodel walks out with this much bourbon, and he kind of knowingly looks at the camera like, Yeah. You go, "I want to live that life. I want to be the hero of that story." And the same thing happens in the nonprofit world. We say, "Hey donor, you can be the hero, you can be the savior," and what we've not done is create neighbors. We've created a hero and a victim, and it opens wallets, and it funds programs, but it's abhorrent and it needs to die. We need a better model of storytelling that says "No, no, no, we are going to bring people together," showing that everybody here has something to give and something to receive.

MOORE: Let's talk about the program.

ACUFF: Where do you want me to start? The overview, the economic development, or the why?

MOORE: Let's start with the why.

ACUFF: Simple premise. Jesus says, "love your neighbor as you love yourself," which is simple to understand, radically complicated to implement. Because from the minute my feet touch the floor, your feet touch the floor, in the morning, we're trying to figure out, how do I provide resources for me and my family. And you think about that as like, drawing a circle of love around you guys. And Jesus says that's great, do that. But if that's all you're doing, it's way too small. It's got to be bigger. So don't just obsess about your kids' educational future, obsess about your neighbors' kids. Don't just think about your own bank account, right. Because on average, how many times a week do you think you check your online banking?

MOORE: If its seven days in a week at least seven times.

ACUFF: I checked it I think three times this morning. I was like, did the money come in or not? Can we make that run to Target? And we're meant to be as concerned about our neighbor's economic future as we are about our own. So that's the why.

MOORE: Many of us are definitely not thinking like that.

ACUFF: No, no, but that's the call of Christ. So I would say if you are a Christian, if you were professing to follow Jesus, your life needs to be about this. Not just as a one-time-only thing, but as a lived-out experience. That doesn't mean we get it perfect, or always right, because we're not floating above the ground. We're complicated people. But we are meant to be aimed in the direction of our neighbor. So that's the why, right.

If you look at Nashville, like most major cities in the US, our Black neighbors have one-eighth the financial stability of our white neighbors. And that's true across all other demographics. This is from a report from the Federal Reserve from 2019. The data is there, backs this up. So the question is what do we do about it, right? Well, there's multiple economic solutions. There's higher wages. There's new job markets. There's training to get jobs at Oracle, whatever. There's lots of different ways to get at that, but I think one of the critical ways is on neighbors' own terms. Having lived in the community, when I saw neighbors doing three to five different things to make their economic year work, the myth of like the lazy person in the hood . . . it's nonsense. That was a Reagan talking point. The reality is, "Oh no, Ms. Kelley over here is doing three to five things and she's gonna make it work." So how do you take one of those things and using basic business, foundational ideas, grow that, and help her to find success? It goes back to the asset base thing.

From a practical standpoint, what that looks like is we have two big categories. It's called the Academy. There's the Primary Academy, which is a ten-week program using this curriculum we licensed that's now used in eighty cities, but we are their number one customer. So, we're the biggest in the nation with that curriculum, where it gives you all the things you need to know in terms of who's your target client? What problem are you solving for them? Who's your competition? How do you get them to know and trust you (a.k.a., marketing)? What are going to be your startup costs, ongoing cost, legal structure? We get into all of that. Then, we bring in guest speakers every week to increase both your knowledge base and your network, because we know network is linked to net worth. If we're going to break down economic segregation, we actually have to get people together. So there's a lot of that.

Then we graduate this with this massive block party, like the in-person one prior to COVID had over five hundred neighbors there. And it feels like a family reunion mixed with a business expo, mixed with a compassionate pitch contest. And when I say that, I mean this is the opposite of *Shark Tank*, the opposite of Silicon Valley. And what I mean by that is like, we do need high-growth companies, I think they're important. They can employ a lot of people, but the framework and the thinking doesn't work for front-porch businesses because that mentality says, You better be incredible and your idea better be incredible, because that is what gets you in this room and keeps you in this room.

MOORE: And you have to be able to potentially project, forecast this amount of money.

ACUFF: Absolutely. All those things. And what we're saying instead is, "Know what gets you in this room and keeps you in this room, and gives you access to this training. It's because you are our neighbor, and that's incredible. You have value, and now the framework." That approach has led to what I would describe as like an empathy-based model, over a competition-based model. So in that one class, you'll see, "Oh, I build websites," "Awesome, I do events," and "Oh I need a logo," and whatever . . . it starts mixing it up, and they're helping each other and their businesses are starting to grow.

And we've got lived examples out of that, like Carlos Partee, who with his co-founder launched the Black Market. He's a graduate and a leader at the Academy, because the classes are led by graduates and they are community located. So they're happening in family rec centers, resource centers, historic neighborhood churches, and we're all over the place. But then, like, Danielle McGee, who launched Black Business Boom. She's a graduate and a teacher, and after teaching one of the academy classes she saw all these business owners who needed access to more clients and access to technology, and she started Black Business Boom.

MOORE: Wow, I didn't know that.

ACUFF: Beautiful things have come out of that model. All you're doing is giving them a framework that's gonna let them unlock some rocket fuel, but it's not about me, and it's not about Corner to Corner. We're going like, big vision. There's national data that says in Nashville we have room for ten thousand more Black-owned businesses. That would be $250 million in the annual economy from the ground up. So we want to make Nashville with partners—with some amazing people we partner with, not us, but in community—we want to make Nashville the number one city to launch or grow a Black-owned business in the South.

MOORE: What does power mean to you? Jesus had a lot of power. The United States military has a lot of power. Sometimes the word *power* can seem threatening because of how we have experienced it or seen how people use their power. So, what do you think about power, and how do you use the power that you have to better community?

ACUFF: I think one of the best things I've read on this is a book called *Strong and Weak* by Andy Crouch. He's a theologian and Christian thinker. I really recommend checking out that book, but one of the things he talks about, as in how Jesus used power, was that he had vulnerability mixed with authority, and that when those are both happening some beautiful flourishing can happen. But when you get authority with no vulnerability, you get, "It's my way or I'll crush you." When it's all vulnerability and no authority, you get poverty. You get people with no voice. Sometimes even in a tragic situation, you get people with neither. Or rather, I'd put it more like this: you get people who give away their authority in order to have a bubble life of fake protection. Think about the strongman: "Vote for this guy because he'll make us feel safer." You're like, "Whoa, like, you bought into the lie?" Crouch's argument is that balance between vulnerability and authority is the sweet spot.

So that's how I personally think about it. Using your power, no matter who you are, for the good of your family and for your neighbor, and using your voice and understanding your voice, and understanding your sphere of influence. Not just for your own good, but also for the good of neighbor. If you have that kind of framework, beautiful things can happen. If instead you're trying to have a protectionist mindset . . . and I see this now. Neighborhoods are gentrifying all over Nashville, all over every urban center in the US. You have almost two types of gentrifiers. I call them the capital *G* and the lower-case *g*. We're all gentrifiers, me too. I bought a house where I could afford it in a low-income neighborhood. I'm a white middle-class guy. I'm a gentrifier. I'd like to think I'm a lower-case *g*.

But a capital-*G* gentrifier is someone who comes in and goes, "I'm going to build the biggest fence. I'm only going to be outside when I have to mow the lawn or unload groceries. I'm not engaging with the neighborhood at all and I'm waiting for it to feel safe to me." That's a castle mentality. That's acting like you're under siege, which is an awful way to live your life. It's not good for you. It's not good for your neighbor. And you're not using any of your power, in your job, in your economic position, to actually learn what's going on in the neighborhood and move toward neighbors. Versus a lower-case-*g* gentrifier, who comes in and goes, "I really want to know my neighbors. I want to know the joys, the sorrows, the highs, the lows. What's going on, let's have a real human relationship." And then you see them automatically start thinking in ways that can benefit their neighbor in a shared experience. Power in that framework can really shift.

MOORE: That was beautifully put. Don't be a capital *G*.

Scan the QR code to watch
the interview with Will Acuff
on YouTube.

PART V

PROTECTION OR HARM

CHAPTER ELEVEN

JORGE SALLES DIAZ

Born in Guatemala City, Jorge has been an organizer in Nashville for the past few years. His organizing home is Workers' Dignity, a workers' center that is organizing within the construction industry for better working conditions and standards.

Jorge takes us into the harm that our Latinx community faces in labor and construction, but also how the indoctrination of white supremacy, which is practiced through anti-Blackness, has caused internal harm within the Latinx community.

In actively trying to create more political education around these issues, Jorge has participated in several projects in Nashville, including Nashville Nonprofit Workers United, Movements Including X, and others. He is currently in law school and is hoping to be a movement lawyer dedicated to supporting immigrant workers.

MOORE: So, Jorge, can you tell us a little bit about your role at Workers' Dignity and what you do and the impact that they have here in Nashville?

DIAZ: Workers' Dignity has been doing grassroots organizing for eleven or so years. But we're at a point where our work is the most exciting that I've felt like in my organizing life for a while. We're trying to create a multiracial base. We're working to unite the people who are traditionally left out of political spaces. Labor movement spaces. We always talk about, Who are your people? In our organizing home, Workers' Dignity, we have the construction campaign because our people are construction workers. We have the Black National Assembly. We have several programs as well. We have a program called Workers' Nights. Workers that have had their wages stolen, that have had an accident in the workplace can come.

You know how the laws here in Tennessee are designed. Governor Lee is a construction developer. So he's the one figuring out worker's comp and all those laws. And so the laws are not on the side of the worker, and these are workers that traditionally have been left out of the labor movement. What we're doing effectively and have been doing for a while is building power in those areas. That's our bread and butter, and that's what I'm focusing on right now. Wage theft and people that have been injured at the workplace. And we're not lawyers. We believe that the power is in the worker, and that's how we do things.

MOORE: That's amazing. And Workers' Dignity will show up at your house. They will show up at your job. They get busy. So for people who may not understand, what is a typical protocol or process if a construction worker comes to you all and says, "Hey I'm not getting paid my fair wage" or "I'm not getting the workers compensation because I was injured on the site"? What is that process like?

DIAZ: So our Workers' Nights are on Thursdays, and people just come. If a worker comes and says, "Hey, I was not paid my wages," first we do an intake, you figure out what's going on. You got to get the facts straight, and the construction industry is very complicated. I don't understand it.

So you have a worker working for a subcontractor working for a contractor who's working for a general contractor. So first, it's figuring out what's really going on, and trying to understand who has the power to pay that worker. It's not always the sub-sub-sub-sub contractor here. So our power analysis is, this contractor that paid a contractor to pay a subcontractor to pay the subcontractor, that dude is responsible for everyone working on that site because the reason why that structure still exists is so you don't have to make yourself responsible. There's a million little companies that come in and work and they skip town and don't pay the workers and that's why construction is so cheap right here in Nashville. The amount of codes and regulations that they skip in the process is terrible. So this dude all the way to the top is benefiting from the work of the little guy and then is lying to them. Like, "Oh it's not my responsibility that they didn't pay you." No, it is a structure that you created that facilitates wage theft.

You have the general contractors telling the workers that it is not their responsibility that they got their wages stolen, but then they benefit from that, from the cheap prices that are only possible because of wage theft. So what we do is we do public pressure campaigns and definitely our largest one is Armando's campaign, Armando Arzate.

Armando, he and his crew were doing construction at the Vanderbilt Divinity School back in 2019. They owe them something ridiculous, like seventy thousand dollars. What ended up happening in that case is like, who has the power to pay Armando? It's usually not the dude that hired him. I mean, in that case, we went to the top general contractor who was still pulling funny shit everywhere, and to Vanderbilt, and a lot of Vanderbilt students put a lot of administration pressure on Vanderbilt to pressure this company to get Armando his money.

MOORE: How did you get started in this work? What inspired you to get into organizing and building power in community?

DIAZ: That's a great question. I started reflecting on theories of change in 2019 and 2020 because I didn't have clarity. I knew in my heart that I wanted to do good, which is a liberal thing to say. But I started working in advocacy roles in helping do policy, helping do case management because the bulk of my professional career has been relatively low wage case management work at a nonprofit. Then I started thinking, "Okay, so I'm a case manager." I was helping people that had housing issues. I'm helping people who are tenants, who are being evicted. Or I'm helping people who need to file bankruptcy but it's just overwhelming.

The amount of people that keep coming to you is far more than your organizations here in town are prepared to help. No wonder, because it's not addressing the root cause of these issues.

So then I was like, "I need to get into systemic work," and I went to do what I thought was systemic work through policy and through other means, through electoral means, and I realized that I meant more top-down electoral strategy. You still face some of those issues where you're the one here, helping the little people here, and at the end of the day it's misguided because you have no leverage. I mean, if you're a policy person—not trying to talk shit. We need good policy people. Because if you're a grassroots organizer, you don't necessarily have all the knowledge about what's going inside. We need someone with eyes there. But policy is just begging, man. You don't have leverage, especially in a state like Tennessee that is so extremely fascist, you don't have leverage. So what's the leverage of the worker? Their labor. That deeply resonated with me.

That's the thing that I really like about us is that we're building a multiracial movement, where we know that we are oppressed in different ways but we want to band together. It's not like, "My issues are more important." We're building power. I'll be honest, that's been difficult because there's a lot of internalized anti-Blackness within the Latinx community.

MOORE: I was going to ask you about that. I've lived in Costa Rica. I lived in Paraguay, and I've been in other countries in South and Central America. So I've been in contact with Latinx communities. But I'm not directly from or in that community, so it's really not my issue to speak on, but I would definitely like for you to break it down to us on that anti-Blackness in the Latinx community, so people can just be aware and educated and do more research on it.

DIAZ: Yeah, for sure. It's a lot of unlearning that we got to do because at the end of the day our futures are tied together. We all need liberation and none of us are free until all of us are free. I really actually think that's true. But we have this legacy of colorism. So we had a caste system in Latin America where white people are the top, as usual, because of colonialism. Then you had mixed-race people, and you had Indigenous and Black people at the bottom. You know, what's sad? A lot of Latinx people conceptualize themselves as white. And that's no mistake. The government, the US Census, the category is white Latino. Or I think it's white Hispanic.

MOORE: What does that even mean?

DIAZ: My people, a lot of us like align with whiteness when you think white people give a fuck about us?

MOORE: Why do you think that is? Is it because they have the perception that white is better? I have more opportunities if I conceptualize to being white? Why do you think that is?

DIAZ: My context is Guatemala. That's where I was born and raised. The country is majority Indigenous. I'm not white, but I enjoy white privilege there because of my proximity to whiteness. Because if you're Indigenous or don't speak Spanish your poverty rates are double. Your likelihood of going to college is a fifth of what it otherwise would be. We have twenty million people and I think we have like one or two Congress representatives who are Indigenous, even though more than half the country's Indigenous. So you get tangible material rewards for trying to approximate whiteness. And you also get an ethnic and racial fluidity there. Because what people do then, there's environmental displacement. There's capital displacement. Once you are displaced, you change your clothes. You no longer wear your Maya outfits. You start speaking Spanish, and your kids don't speak your Indigenous language, whether that's Achi or Kaqchikel or any other; we have twenty-six of them. That comes with a material reward. So when we talk about race, at least in my context, in Guatemala, it is embedded in an economic structure. I'm so grateful for the Black community, who has a commitment to stay with us. To move with us. I think it's really beautiful that we're trying to have this multiracial movement. Even though my community has shit to unlearn.

MOORE: What are some ways that the Latinx community is helping to learn or unlearn some of those things that promote white supremacy?

DIAZ: One is political education. I don't think that this can be done standing by itself. If you just go to people and you're like, "Let me talk to you about this," it tends to be not as effective as when you're moving together toward something. So, definitely political education within our movements, and that's not just Workers' Dignity doing that. I don't want to claim credit. We got to do better too. Everyone has to do better.

MOORE: And everybody is growing and trying to do better.

DIAZ: I think the MIX, Movements Including X. Yeah, I think that they're developing an analysis of like, what it means to be Latinx. That includes that legacy of colorism, of racism, and undoing that is crucial to our liberation. That's where we are at, and I'm excited.

Scan the QR code to watch
the interview with George
Salles Diaz on YouTube.

CHAPTER TWELVE

CAPTAIN CARLOS LARA

Many people may find it hard to interact on any level with police. This is where creating a brave space of welcoming and allowing the perspectives of all really comes into play.

Born and raised in Boston, Carlos Lara moved to Nashville, where thousands of newly arrived Latinx people have made their homes. He first started interacting with immigrant communities as a medical assistant at Centennial Pediatrics, whose clients were mostly Kurdish and Mexican children.

Lara left the medical profession when he decided to become a police officer with the Metropolitan Nashville Police Department (MNPD). In this conversation Lara shares his thoughts on how police impact public schools, the debate around police funding, safety, and the historical relationship that police have with some communities.

Carlos is the first Latino captain in the history of MNPD. He serves as the chief diversity officer and MNPD's liaison to the Community Oversight Board (COB).

MOORE: Many people may not know this but Carlos, you're actually the first Latino, Latinx chief diversity officer that MNPD has had.

LARA: Yes, I am blessed. I thank God. I am blessed more than I deserve. It's been unbelievable to be able to see where I'm at now. I was actually the first Hispanic lieutenant. I was the first Hispanic captain, and now Chief Drake, when he was appointed chief, appointed me the chief diversity officer of the department. So again, there's a lot smarter people than I am here in this department. But I'm blessed to be where I'm at. It really gives me a lot of sense of pride to be able to say that I'm able to open doors for others that are in the same place that I was.

MOORE: Being a man of color and always being that *first*, how do you internalize that, especially in the police department, knowing how specifically people of color have had a peculiar relationship with police historically?

LARA: It's an incredible privilege and it's a blessing. It's kind of a double-edged sword, because it's hard, because you're the first. So, you don't really know. You're kind of setting the tone for how things are going to move forward. But at the same time, you're able to set the tone, probably, to move forward and be able to represent not only the Hispanic community, but the minority community in general. It's great because we've had some minorities move up in the past, but I think with Chief Drake now, he's really made it a point to say, "Hey, we need to make sure that our department reflects the community," and so he started to really look at the incredible, talented people of all races, white, Black, Hispanic, Asian. I mean, we've got an incredible group of men and women in our department, but to be able to start kind of that rise of the minorities in the department is awesome. And I think the city's going to really see the fruits of that, and it's going to be a blessing to the city because you're going to have, again, people that are from these neighborhoods that are going to be helping police. These neighborhoods are helping create policies for the neighborhood, for the way that we police. So internalizing it, sometimes I think about it and I'm like, man, I don't know how I got here.

MOORE: So can you break it down for us, what's a day in the life of the chief diversity officer?

LARA: So the chief diversity officer in general in the private sector has always been more internal. They deal with personnel issues within the organizations. My job is a little bit different. Chief diversity officer is the title that I've been given, but what I'm really doing a lot more of is I'm reaching out to diverse communities. I have a lot of interactions with the Kurdish community, the Asian community, the Hispanic community constantly, trying to figure out the Somali community, Muslim, Vietnamese. And so really, reaching out to a lot of these communities that historically haven't had a really good relationship with the department, or have had no relationship with the police department, trying to reach out and let them know, "Hey, we see you, we care about you. We want to serve you." And so a lot of the things that I do is coordinating. A lot of meetings with the leaders in these communities going, "Hey, what are the issues you're having? What can we do to help?"

In the past, a lot of times we used to go as police officers, going to neighborhoods and going, "This is your problem, and I'm going to tell you how I'm going to fix it." We don't do that anymore. Chief Drake has been very, very adamant. "We're going to look and see what the community wants." We're going in and going, "Hey, I see the problem. I've got an idea, but I want to know what your idea is so that we can figure out the best way of attacking this problem and fixing it." So it's a lot of conversation. It's a lot of education, and a lot of really, just letting people know that we care. Engage with them, be part of their events, invite them to our events, and just really try to start building that partnership relationship with these communities. So that's a lot of what I do. This position, also the liaison to community oversight board, that's the first liaison we've ever had. So that's another dynamic to the position I'm in.

I think sometimes there's a misunderstanding that the COB and the MNPD have two different desires, or they have two different goals. Our goals are really the same. We don't want bad officers in our department. The people who hate bad officers more than everybody else is good officers. Because the bad officers give such a bad name to the good officers. Now the good officers have to deal with all the backlash from things that they had nothing to do with, so we don't want bad officers here. We don't want them. If you're not going to serve the people, if you're not going to do what's right, go somewhere else. And I think that we both have that goal. It's just that we're looking at it from two different eyes.

MOORE: This is the educational piece. I think everybody would agree all police officers are not bad police officers. It's more the system historically, especially when it comes to people of color, of what the larger picture has been, and statistics to prove these things right. I think like the prison population now is, as far as when it comes to just Black men alone, is over 50 percent. If we include Latinx and Black it definitely makes up a majority of the prison population. And we're a minority of the United States population. How are we meeting these disparities?

When it comes to policies, once a bad officer has been identified, it seems like a lot of people have a problem with the protocols that are in place to prevent them ever policing again, because they can move to another city, another state. And it seemed like it's a lack of transparency or a clearinghouse. That person was being discriminatory toward a group of people. That's why they were fired. Why are they able to get another job?

LARA: There's policies, there're laws, things that need to be followed. For us there's the POST [Peace Officer Standards & Training Commission], the organization that certifies us. We get our POST certifications through Tennessee. If somebody gets fired for some reason, we understand that we have to let the POST know this officer got fired and then they can go ahead and see if they revoked their certification. So they'd have to go somewhere else. "Hey, are you POST certified?" "Well, no, I was. I'm not POST certified because I got pulled by the certification organization or body." And then they go, "Well, why'd you get it pulled?" "Well, I got it pulled because of x y z." A lot of times, some of the other departments don't do that background that they need to. They don't do the thorough check that needs to be done. And there's got to be a better way of doing it because again, there's a lot of disconnects within the different organizations. The more you connect, the more you're able to work together to get this information so everybody's on the same page, I think it's easier. I think legislation is coming through that is making it a little bit easier to identify problem officers or problem police personnel that leave and try to get a job somewhere else. We need to go ahead and really do a good background check and go, "Let's go talk to the department. Let's go figure out your personnel file. Let's go ahead and talk to POST, and get that information before a decision is made to hire somebody."

MOORE: See, people like myself are not going to be familiar with that process. Having you break that down, I think is going to really help people look more into it, like, "Oh, it's the POST that needs to be getting on their job more and regulating some of these things," specifically here in Tennessee.
    Let's talk about budget a little bit.

LARA: Okay.

MOORE: Police budget, money. As a community organizer, we are always thinking like, Where can we get funds to put into other areas as needed for the community? Here in Nashville it's a huge conversation when it comes to how much money is MNPD is getting. What is this money going to? Why do they need so much? Why do we need more SROs [school resource officers]? Why do we need more police officers? Why do we need a helicopter? Why do we need these things? So I'm going to throw out some trigger words for you. When you hear "reimagine police funding," or "defunding police," what does that mean to you?

LARA: I completely agree with reimagining how policing is done. I don't think policing done twenty, thirty years ago is very different than what needs to be done today. I think fifty years ago, sixty years ago, the way things were done is very different than today, and they should be done differently. When I think of defunding, I don't really think people understand where our funds go. The majority of our funds go to police personnel, salaries. It's like 75 percent goes to that. And when you think about the city and how it's grown, we've got close to seven hundred thousand people here. We're pretty much policing with the same amount that we policed, I think, twenty years ago, which was like 1,300 officers. We've got about that much right now and a city our size should have probably close to 1,800, 2,000 officers just because of the area. We've got five hundred and, I think, thirty-plus square miles. All of the events that we have here take manpower.

A lot of times people look at it and go "Well, we're doing a lot of policing." But you know, we're going out there stopping cars, this and that, but I don't know if they realize all of the other things that we have to do, such as all of the traffic issues downtown, these big events, Fourth of July, New Year's, the NFL draft that came. That is a huge amount of personnel that is necessary to keep the city safe. I think this past event that we had had 250,000, 300,000 people that showed up. The draft had 600,000. We've got to make sure that people are safe and it takes manpower. I'm all about making sure that other initiatives and other programs have the funding, but I don't think that taking them away from one that's already underfunded, to be honest with you, compared to what we need, and give it to somebody else is going to help.

MOORE: That's going to blow people's minds. The police are underfunded.

LARA: Let me tell you, if you look at all the things that we need, that would make it safer. Training and all of this. I mean, again, you're talking about 70 percent is just the personnel. Just salaries, benefits, things like health insurance, things like that. And then you're talking about all of the different technologies, the different training that comes out. That all costs money.

MOORE: People are going to say, "Hey, police get all this money. It can be going more to housing. It can be going more to community organizations." For example, when it comes to funding for SROs. Why not have school professional counselors instead of police officers? We had Safer Schools on here to talk about that a little bit and I told them Carlos would be on here to talk probably a little more deeply. It seems like, with SROs and MNPD, that principals, school leadership, have one understanding on what they're there to do and MNPD has another different understanding of what they're there to do. You have school leadership asking SROs to do things that they're really not there to really do, but can get involved in. When it comes to budget, let's put more people back in policing on the street . . . if it's in demand, let's get those individuals fighting crime and doing those things and get school counselors in there instead. That's just one conversation I know, when you're talking budget and reimagining or defunding specifically.

LARA: Well, I think one of the things that people may not understand is that we are not actually getting extra money for our SROs. This is just part of our budget. And the chief just says, "I'm going to take these officers, I'm gonna put them in schools because I think that that's an important place for them to be." So it's not that we're getting extra money specifically, "Hey, this is funding that you're getting for SROs." The chief can take all these SROs out of the schools if he wanted to and put them somewhere else, but he feels it's very important to have somebody there. Not only to protect kids, because of different things that have happened in the past. We could look at history and see all the terrible incidents that have occurred in different schools. Being able to have somebody there to help address those issues as soon as possible . . . that's a whole other conversation, but I think that when you're looking at SROs, everybody has their own thoughts.

The schools started to ask SROs to do things that aren't what we're there for. Enforcing house rules, "This child right here, he doesn't want to listen." That's not our job. Our job is to protect if there's a criminal issue where a specific crime has been committed. We're not there to be teacher bodyguards. "If something bad happens, you call the police officers, they'll take care of it." No, that's not our job.

Really we want to help kids understand who we are and to feel comfortable around police. So when they get outside and they see them on the street, they don't have that fear. So there's different roles that the officers use as SROs, mentoring some of these kids. There's certain things that they will tell the SROs that they won't tell their teachers, and certain issues that are occurring that they may not feel comfortable telling the teacher, but they will say, "Hey, SRO so-and-so,

I've got an issue. Can you help me?" Our focus on SROs in schools is to build relationship with the kids. To protect first of all, but to build those relationships with kids so that when they leave, they don't have that fear of officers. Now again, when the teacher, if somebody says, "Hey, this child is acting up, you need to call the SRO." That's not our place. That's not what we're there for. That's the issue. They have been utilized in a way that they shouldn't be utilized.

MOORE: What would you say to the parent or person who says, "Hey, I don't think school is the best place for my child to be building a relationship with police officers"?

LARA: My question would be, where is the best place to build a relationship with police officers? Now, I'm not saying that schools is the perfect place, but how are they going to build a relationship outside of the school? Are they going to build a relationship when they're stopped or if they have interactions on the street? That's not really relationship. Maybe an interaction. That's a great question.

I think that again, we're using the form that we have available to try to make a difference. And is it always going to be perfect? No. But I think that we're using what we can, and I think that being able to be in schools is kind of a double-pronged thing. We're there to protect if something happens and be a deterrent. "Hey, there's an SRO there, you know, you may not want to go in there and do anything." But also, hey, there's kids here that we can maybe impact. We're going to interact with them and have that positive interaction with them. That someone may go home, they could say, "Mom, Dad, you know, not all police officers are bad." "Hey, I met so-and-so and he was cool and he treated me right," and this and that. "I'm not afraid of police when I go out and see them on the street."

MOORE: I know I said this earlier, there is no way you can say all police officers, because you're talking individuals, are bad. It's a system and then it's risk assessment, right? I know Captain Lara, and I know all police officers are not bad, but I also know, historically, me getting pulled over is going to be maybe a little bit different. I have to have different mannerisms. I shouldn't have to, but that's just the reality of what we've seen, that I can go off of historically, so that I can make it back home to my family. That just is what it is in this country. So I think those interactions, those historical interactions to the present day . . . I think that is causing a lot of pause when it comes to building relationships in general, whether in school, whether in community. Because of the damage and trauma that a lot of us have faced. I might want to trust, but something happens to a person that looks like me or comes from the same area that I'm from and I'm just like, "I can't do it." I'm glad I'm having this conversation with you because it could happen to you. People may not know that you're the chief diversity officer and you could be a victim of that same type of discrimination.

LARA: Absolutely. There is no doubt in my mind whatsoever that policing was done in a different way and it really hurt a lot of people. There's a lot of people out there now that were around in the '60s, '70s, when policing was just like another world, and they are still traumatized by a lot of those things, and it still affects them and those experiences have now been passed down to kids, grandkids, great grandkids. And so what grandma and grandpa remember is what they're telling their kids now, and those kids are going "Well that's what's happening. My mind is that that is what it's like now."

We are moving into a different type of policing, and I think it's pretty clear across the country when you're seeing how people are changing the way they're policing. Here in Nashville, the chief has been very clear. We got rid of a bunch of our proactive units. We used to have Flex units. They're the unmarked cars that use to stop everybody. Those are gone. We used to have crime-suppression units, which used to be the plainclothes drug narcotics officers on the streets. They were out there doing drug busts. And all types of drug investigations, prostitution investigations, they're gone. Now we're replacing them with Community Engagement Teams, teams that are not out there trying to police the way that people have always seen policing. They're out there saying, "I want to start building a relationship."

We want to start engaging the community, connecting with them and letting them really know that we're not here to hurt you. We want you to feel comfortable with us. We want you to feel protected when we're around. We've got a long way to go, don't get me wrong, but I think we're taking steps to get there. It's not going to be an overnight fix, it cannot be a one-year fix, not a two-year fix. It's going to be a long-term fix that we have to continue to build that trust. I think that is why we have Community Engagement Teams. The office that I supervise, the Office of Community Outreach and Partnerships, which is under the chief's office, is there to reach out to those immigrant communities, a lot of the underserved communities that historically have been afraid of the police. They don't understand the way policing is done, so we're trying to change that.

Are we going to do it perfectly? No, it's going to be just like anything else. There's going to be things that we're going to do wrong. We're looking at different ways to do it better and that's why we need the input of the communities we serve. And that's what we're getting, that change of tide, the way we police differently here. Because I can tell you right now, we police very differently today than we did even a year ago.

MOORE: A lot of people are not familiar with protocol and training when it comes to stops and things like that. When somebody dies, from the lens of a resident it doesn't seem like that officer should have pulled out his or her gun. Why didn't they use a taser? From an MNPD perspective, what are your thoughts on that, when it comes to using a firearm compared to a taser, and what should residents know about the training and policy procedures when it comes to that? Because a lot of times he or she shouldn't have been shot. They shouldn't have been killed for that, especially when there's a mental illness involved.

LARA: There's always things we can do better, always. You're never going to be a perfect department. As times evolve, as policing evolves, there's always going to be new things that we can do better, no doubt. Some of the things that the public may not know is the training. We get about twenty-six weeks of training at the training academy. A trainee goes in and gets the background checks, gets accepted to the police department. They go for about twenty-six weeks now, more training now than we did in the past, to get trained to learn all of the rules, the laws, the other things, the foundation that they need to be a police officer.

They do, I think, two weeks of firearms. They do taser training and use of force. I mean, all these different things. Then they go do six months of field training. They go with a field training officer and learn how to apply the things they've learned at the Academy into real life situations. I personally, and I don't think I've ever met an officer that's ever wanted to pull the trigger. I know that because of what we see on the news, people think, "Man, the officers wake up in the morning ready to pop a round off." I can tell you that that's not realistic. It may seem it, because all we see in the media is the really bad situations. There are bad officers, like I said, 100 percent there are bad officers out there, and we don't want them around. But the majority of the officers are good people and they care about the communities, and they don't want to do that.

The issue that you have sometimes is the situation. It's all situational. You know, I don't know what's going on through that officer's mind. I don't know what he's seeing. I don't know why situations can go from zero to sixty like that. When you look at the training, we ask, "Is the officer following the training and is he following the law?" Every time a life is taken, it's a terrible thing. Whether it's a good person or a bad person, you know, it's a terrible thing. It's a life that's taken . . . because it doesn't just affect them, it affects their families. It affects everybody else. Sometimes hindsight is 20/20. You may not agree with why somebody did something, but there's a lot of aspects of it that you have to look at. You got to look at the human aspect of it.

I've heard this a lot: "Why didn't they shoot the gun out of their hand, or why didn't they shoot them in the leg?" I don't think that people realize that that is not a realistic thing that we can do. There are some really good shooters out there, but there are so many things that affect being able to shoot somebody in the leg or in the arm. "Why didn't they use the taser?" When you look at those things, you have to ask, is that a realistic thing that they can actually do? I can tell you, there's no officer that's going to be able to pop rounds off and go, "I'm going to shoot him in the leg." "I'm going to shoot a round down and see what happens." Every round that comes out of our firearm we have to be accountable for. If I'm just starting to try to hit someone in the leg, and I hit somebody behind them or somebody like that, we're now accountable for that. It's not easy to do those things. It's not realistic. People may go, "You got to get trained." I don't care how much training you have, when adrenaline is rushing, when you're moving, all these different factors are happening, those are not realistic.

Apart from those things, I think that understanding that the taser doesn't always work. The taser only works up to probably 60 to 70 percent of the time, because it all depends on clothing. It depends if they connected the taser connectors. So many different things. A lot of times we've had officers utilize tasers and they didn't work. What do you do now? Somebody has a knife coming at you, and you try to tase them and it doesn't work . . . it's such a difficult situation to be in, and I don't think any officer wants to be in it, but it's something that when you're in the situation, you sometimes react with how you've been trained or sometimes you act with what's inside of you. I think that we train as much as you can. We're constantly trying to evolve with our training. We do a lot of de-escalation, that is key right now, and that's what we really focused on. Even Chief Anderson focused on it, but Chief Drake is focused on it even more. De-escalation. Why are we going one hundred miles an hour on this? Slow down, figure out what we can do. Yes, that person has a weapon, but is anybody here in immediate danger of losing a limb or of serious bodily injury or death? No. So let's back off, figure out what we can do to end this in a peaceful manner so nobody gets injured. That is one of the big keys that we're doing now, is slow it down. We don't need to rush into situations. In the past we did that a lot, and I think that Chief Drake has said we're going to slow it down and we're going to start using other resources that we have before we start pulling out those weapons.

MOORE: To close us out, Carlos. Where do you see the future of policing and community engagement with policing here in Nashville?

LARA: I'll tell you, the goal that we have is to be a partnership. We want this to be a city where I don't care where you're from. I don't care how much money you make. I don't care what kind of job you have. I'll give you Black, white, Hispanic, whatever. You should feel that you're being treated with dignity, respect, by every officer. You should feel that you should not be afraid of talking to an officer or coming up to them when you need help, and you should be given the resources that you need. Not just by the officer, by everyone, for all of our citizens. No matter what culture you are.

Scan the QR code to watch
the interview with Captain
Carlos Lara on YouTube.

CHAPTER THIRTEEN

MARCUS TROTTER-LOCKETT AND EMMA CROWNOVER OF SAFER SCHOOLS NASHVILLE

Many people believe the presence of police officers in our schools would make them safer, right? Safer Schools representatives Marcus Trotter-Lockett and Emma Crownover have different thoughts about police being in schools.

Safer Schools is a community organization working toward safer alternatives to school police officers and advancing the social, emotional, and intellectual development of all Metro Nashville Public Schools (MNPS) students.

MOORE: You're a new organization. Break down who Safer Schools Nashville is, your mission and purpose, and then we can get into like some meaty, possibly controversial things that you all are trying to advocate for in the city of Nashville.

TROTTER-LOCKETT: It's pretty much all been tested by the trauma of 2020. That was a bad year for all of us. I was in college in California, I wasn't here. After George Floyd, there was a large call. We're all ex-MNPS students. All of us went to Hume Fogg. We were in the same grade at Hume Fogg. A lot of the adults who work with us were also grades above us, or around the same grade at Hume Fogg. So there was a kind of a call to action after George Floyd. It was a real conversation about, we don't like what our country looks like. We don't like what the world around us looks like, what can we do as people who care to change that? And that was the beginnings of what's now been a year and a half, which blows my mind, of Safer Schools.

We stole FUBU—for students by students—our idea was as ex-students in MNPS, how can we advocate for the social, emotional, and mental well-being of students, to work toward advocating for their needs during the pandemic? The biggest thing is, how do we approach this with the metro schools in a way that is best for students? Including removing school resource officers (SROs) from schools, including reallocating money toward more beneficial programs for students within schools, and kind of having a perspective of saying that these kids spend their entire lives in MNPS before college, and they have no say in anything involved.

So how, as an organization, could we give back in some way to the people we think are most vulnerable within schools during a tumultuous time in this country? And students, you know that clichéd phrase, "are the future," but they can't be anything if they have no voice. So that's kind of where we came from, what we're about. And we've been on that for, I don't think any of us expected, a year and a half.

MOORE: I'm curious, what made you want to get involved?

CROWNOVER: I think that it is important to note that we aren't in high school anymore. COVID gave us this free time, and the movement of George Floyd and everything that happened after that gave us this momentum, but it is rooted in our high school experience, in our education in Nashville. We all grew up in Nashville. We all went to MNPS schools our whole lives. But the really unique thing about going to a school downtown is that it's not a zoned school, so we came from all over Nashville and we come from very different perspectives, but we are all noticing the same problem. The moment that it happened for me was when, I think I was talking to Cozar, and we were talking about how other cities are having these movements where they're getting cops out of schools and they get to go to public schools that don't have police in them, whether or not having a cop has been specifically harmful to someone, but just neutrally having that be something that our city is investing in. And I think we just had this moment where we like, "we deserve to have that too, and our city deserves to have that too." If we have to go to school and have these other professionals there with the actual tools that help our students, that's something that we want to advocate for . . . for the people that come after us.

MOORE: What have some of the students said are some of the things that they are facing in MNPS schools?

TROTTER-LOCKETT: I think the biggest thing worn away by COVID in a very, very, negative way is support. We talked about having the requisite number of nurses or school counselors, psychologists . . . having someone who can replace an officer to deal with social stigma, things like that. We have a question we used to ask at workshops with students. "Who is your biggest network of support at your school?" And the answer was always one of two things: teacher or a coach. That's awesome. You know, I had relationships like that when I was in school. They were life changing for me, and important.

What would be interesting about that is you can have, in one meeting, three or four kids say the same teacher's name. Which then said to me, "Okay, there's about, I don't know, eight hundred kids in that school, nine hundred kids at school. So how many more after those three or four kids are saying her name?" And that's been something where it seems pretty straightforward that we want our kids to be supported and uplifted in the best way possible in their school. Because that's the place of learning, a place where they're supposed to be cultivating their futures, you know, not only through education but building themselves as people. And we don't seem to have any push to do that, and that's been something that's been brought up a bunch during COVID especially.

We had meetings, Mayor's Youth Council, which is an organization of students who kind of interact with the mayor . . . we had noted in conversations that certain schools that are considered to be, kind of, more problematic, which I hate to use that term because I think that's the wrong way to associate it, but just based on how MNPS categorizes, more problematic schools when it comes to discipline. And the biggest thing was, "I have no one to talk to when I'm in trouble. I have no one to have a conversation with, when I need help with college." Or "I have a teacher who will talk to me or help me, but there are twenty-five other students in her class at the same time at lunch because who else are they going to talk to?" And that's just something I think is unfortunate. I think even worse, it's normalized. I think we bring up having the normal amount of nurses, psychologists, and school counselors and people kind of scoff at that because they're like, "Yeah, we're close," and I'm like, "Oh, that's not enough."

MOORE: I'm interested in knowing what our school board is doing or not doing.

TROTTER-LOCKETT: I'll give my politician's disclaimer at the outset, just to kind of save my own ass. COVID has complicated things a lot. I think we understand that. I think there's a lot of good things that happened in this past budget cycle that improved things. SEL wasn't fully funded, which is Social Emotional Learning, but it's the highest it's been in . . . I think ever. Teachers got a pay raise. There was an increase in investment for teachers, especially for veteran teachers. They got an even higher pay rate than new teachers. And there was commitment by the mayor and the council supporting the school board about having a continued influx of funding for schooling over the next two budget cycles. Those are two big important issues. Now, that being said, that is a Band-Aid on a gunshot wound. And that's something where we have had an issue, is it's been a big pass-the-buck contest. We started out with the school board and they said, "Hey, we can love what you guys are trying to do, this is great work on this. You guys are going to go far with this, go talk to, you know, the council." We go to the council, the council says, "This is great, it's awesome. The mayor has the discretion budget, go talk to the mayor." Then "Cooperate with the police office. They have discretion, so go talk with the police." That was three, four, five meetings and we were back to the council. They're like, "Oh, yeah, this, you know, people are interested if you are interested." I think before the budget was passed there was a bill introduced. I don't remember the exact details of the bill, but I think was just reallocating funding from SROs.

No one wants to take that stance, being the person who's pushed that movement forward of getting rid of SROs. We all try to explain to people it's just one facet of an issue, getting rid of SROs. The ideal is reallocating funding in specific ways. The idea of having the specific investment in mental well-being, mental health in schools, and programs to deal with that. And that's something that's not as simple as just remove cops. There's ideas we talk about . . . students, one of the ideas from students—this is from people in the Mayor's Youth Council—was what if we had a mental health center in the middle of downtown any student can have a key card to get into? There would be counselors there and any student could show up whenever they wanted to. I'm not saying that that's something that's going to happen or has to happen. A student said that in a meeting with the mayor. I've heard nothing about it since. What frustrates us is there is a political calculation: "What is the worst if I do this, what is the worst if I do nothing?" I think people keep skewing toward that latter answer of "I could do nothing and still kind of get away with this, not be a huge issue for me."

The issue that pisses me off is there's a lack of respect for the capacity and ability of students to be human. I think there's a demonizing aspect. A wrangling of animals more than dealing with actual people. I think once you understand that someone is upset for a specific reason, and that's to deal with things at home or who works, who has to take care of a sibling, who has just as much of these stressors as we do as adults, or almost approaching that level . . . I think you have to create programs that aren't to mitigate the annoyance of that situation you're put in as a principal or a teacher—or I guess even an SRO—but think, "I have to mitigate a situation of a human being who's in crisis or in trouble." I think that's the issue we run into, is programs exist, and there are multitudes. It's not just like we're advocating for one. There's a multitude to choose from, and they're all better than a police man who has quite literally jurisdiction over the entire school with no boss above.

MNPS has a memorandum of understanding with Metro Police, and that's about it. The jurisdiction within schools are officers' controlled by MNPD. The comings and goings of officers, what they're going to do in those schools, is controlled by MNPD. So we have talked to principals, who have talked about, "I've had students who've been fighting, or have something that's gone on where they had to be sent to my office be dealt with, and I've said, 'This is yada yada who has this trouble in his life. We know about their struggle. I'm his principal, this is his teacher. We both know this. We know where we're way more well-versed than you.'" and the SRO has been like, "I don't care. We're arresting and he's going to jail." And that's something they have the discretion to do. If we're okay with that then there is a deeply, deeply seated issue in this district.

MOORE: My thing is, with MNPD, where are the stats or the facts that proves that your presence is beneficial?

CROWNOVER: I think that's the most frustrating thing, is that they don't have to prove it. We're all over here doing all this calculus to try and be like, "97 percent of our students that are getting arrested have a disability." But they don't have to prove that their presence . . . It's all emotional.

MOORE: How can Safer Schools get more kids organized?

TROTTER-LOCKETT: That's been the hardest part about the timing when we kind of began as a group. As an organization, that public action was almost impossible during COVID.

MOORE: We're back outside now.

TROTTER-LOCKETT: We now have the ability to change that. It wasn't a thing where the momentum was lacking or it was never here. I'm not going to ask any kid who's sat in his room all day listening to his teacher while taking care of his sister and has a job, "Hey, Nick, can you . . ."

Now that we are out of that, the idea is getting on a level where there's two students now who have officially become honorary school board members, who have a nonvoting kind of say and a student opinion when it comes to the school board. I think the idea of having public events, having face-to-face conversations, having the ability to have the conversation with students in a public forum where we can work with them, saying, "Hey, this is what we're about. This is what we're trying to advocate for you. One, is this what you want? And two, if this is what you want, here are the ways we know to do it."

I think most of us are not amazing, fantastic super organizers like you, Jerome, but we're pretty literate on what it takes to have public action campaigns. Here's your options, to students, to do certain things to get your voices heard and get that out there. We are here to be a resource to help you do that. Now we can be outside again, because we're working right now to encapsulate what all the issues are and kind of make them public and then create a movement of students around that.

Like I said, think the idea of having a report that we can hold, and also create a movement of students around that is the goal. We have to reckon with the fact of this. It's something that's going to have to be dealt with, because Nashville is changing at such a rate and we're dealing with these walls being put up and these gaps and disparities being so exacerbated throughout the city as we had this huge influx population, economic change based on our changing kind of economy . . . we're a tourist economy now, which kind of blows my mind. People are going to get so left behind. That's what worries me about things like this. If we don't deal with them soon, they're going to become something where there are issues that will not only not be dealt with, but dealt with too late.

CROWNOVER: When we first started this, realizing this has been an issue since before we were alive, that the way that we discipline our students in Nashville is above and beyond any other place, and the way we arrest our students in schools. The way we go about discipline is something that has been an issue for years and years and years and nothing has happened. And I think that drove a lot of our work. Like, why is there a 2003 report that says the same exact things that we're talking about? Why has it been my entire life and nothing has changed? Where do we go from here? How do we build people power, because these politicians are sending us in circles. How do we connect with parents? How do we get administrators on board? Because alternative programs don't work if the principal is not on board. And that's what we've seen at some of these high schools that have restorative justice, but not everybody is on board. So this has become a little bit of a joke and it's just like, why can't we do something about this?

Scan the QR code to watch
the interview with Marcus Trotter-
Lockett and Emma Crownover of
Safer Schools Nashville on YouTube.

ACKNOWLEDGMENTS

I would like to acknowledge my vast and amazing community of supporters that encouraged me to explore and played a major role of getting me to this point in my life in Nashville, Tennessee; Peace Corps Paraguay; Puerto Jimenez, Costa Rica; Xiamen, China; and Bacolod, Philippines.

I would not have been able to do this without the vision and continual support of my editor, Zack Gresham. I appreciate all the nudges.

I want to mention my son, Jamieson Moore. One day you will be able to read this and know that seeing you every day motivated and inspired me to complete this book. I want you to never stop exploring life, communities, and the perspectives of those around the world.

Of course, this book would not be what it is without all the amazing people who made themselves available to have a conversation with me. That includes those who are in the book and those who are not. I appreciate you all for your thoughts and time.